T0354545

JESUS

MY BELOVED CONNECTION
TO HUMANITY AND THE SEA

Narrator: Jesus/Jeshua ben Joseph

Rev. Cynthia Williams

&

Verling CHAKO Priest, Ph.D.

Revised Edition

Order this book online at www.trafford.com
or email orders@trafford.com

Most Trafford titles are also available at major online book retailers.

Cover layout by Authors & Graphic-Artist, Adam Miller Schwartz. Photo: Twelve Apostles Sea Stacks,
Great Ocean Road, Victoria, Australia. Legally purchased through www.istockphoto.com/store
Order ID: #12146394

Printed in the United States of America.

ISBN: 978-1-4669-7641-2 (sc)
ISBN: 978-1-4669-7642-9 (hc)
ISBN: 978-1-4669-7640-5 (e)

Library of Congress Control Number: 2013900515

Trafford rev. 01/18/2013

 www.trafford.com

North America & international
toll-free: 1 888 232 4444 (USA & Canada)
phone: 250 383 6864 ✦ fax: 812 355 4082

I dedicate this book to humanity, my brothers and sisters,
and your full awakening to the Light
and the Gods that
You are.
Jesus/Jeshua ben Joseph.

ACKNOWLEDGMENTS

Cynthia: I thank the Heavens for allowing me to take part in this project. I give my love to my brother Jesus/Jeshua ben Joseph and all of the Oceans and the Cetaceans. Your love for humanity amazes me. May all awaken to who they are and why they are here.

To my writing companion, Chako Priest, there are no words to express my appreciation to you for your help in this project. My sister, I love you.

Thank you, Heather, for your wonderful editing and to all others who helped get this book into print.

I wish to thank humanity, as I have been blessed to see through Jeshua's eyes his great love for all. Thank you for my own wake-up!

And last, my gratitude to my unseen Heavenly friends . . . I love you!

Chako: From my heart to your heart, Jesus/Jeshua, and with the deepest appreciation, I thank you for the privilege to be of service to you and God.

Cynthia Williams, my past-life sister, is a superb channel. This book would not have been possible without her beautiful gifts and dedication to Jeshua's request. I thank you with much love.

Heather, we could not have done this without your editing—from commas to whatever else an editor finds. For you Beloveds who may not know, Heather Clarke is the founder of the Arizona Enlightenment Center. She is our *Energizer Bunny*, as she just keeps going and going to the wee hours in the morning in order to finish our chapters. I thank you, dear heart, for all that you do.

Susan Verling Miller O'Brien, my oldest daughter, frames the books for me. I send her the material and voila, our book is formed. I keep saying I am going to learn how to put the Table of Contents together but then never seem to get around to learning the task. Therefore, once again, my dearest heart, you have formed a book for us. Thank you!

Adam Miller Schwartz is my grandson and lives outside of Boston, MA. He is a superb graphic artist. He always comes up with beautiful ideas for space and color. I think you will agree his work for the cover of this book is beyond wonderful. I thank you, dear one, for your soul-felt work.

I offer a special thanks to Joseph Endriss. He tapes all of Jeshua/ Cynthia's lectures and makes them available on CDs to the public. He also transcribed a short segment in chapter 9 for me when my recorder did not register Jeshua's remarks about his lineage—my deepest appreciation, dear friend.

Beloveds, a book is only as successful as there are people who will read it! You have been steadfast in your reading of my books. Thank you for your support and e-mail comments. Cynthia and I will be much interested in reading your remarks after you read Jesus/ Jeshua's book and now this revised edition!

Blessings to all, Chako (2013).

CONTENTS

PREFACE

Chako's Remarks: Hello dear Beloveds, here I am again writing the Preface for my/our next book. For those of you who have read my last book, *The Goddess Returns to Earth*, you know that the Presenters frequently spoke of my collaborating with another author, Cynthia Williams, who is a voice-channel. Well, it has happened, and she will be adding her remarks to mine shortly.

Jeshua has asked me to include his quote here: *"I came through two mediums, one conscious* (Chako-telepathic) *and one as a trance voice-medium* (Cynthia), *to bring my story to the forefront—a story that has not been fully revealed. I am taking a very narrow perspective from humanity and stretching it out."*

From the get-go, Jeshua told me that Cynthia and I were sisters, and he was our brother in that past life. He wanted the book to be written in the Trinity energy of three, so he has come and brought us all under the same umbrella.

You will notice that I am now spelling Yeshua with a **J** as in Jeshua, for I had asked him how he wished his name to be spelled for the book (since I am the scribe). He said that the **Y** was the spelling for his Hebrew name in that lifetime. *"It will lock the book into an energy paradigm* (Hebrew of antiquity) *if I use the Y."* He has left that past life of over 2000 years ago. By spelling his name with a **J** now, I have taken him out of that box of antiquity, which allows humanity to see him through a broader lens and *"that finally gets me off the pedestal."*

You will notice that the format of this book is different from my previous books. Jeshua and I will no longer have our little conversations before and after each chapter. "*This book is important to read as a story-line. It is to contain the heart. If we get too much into **our** dialogue, it takes away from the rhythm of the book. You have been talking to me about this book over and over and over again. We have sat down and have had many talks, as has Cynthia. I have chosen you two to bring my story through, for it has not been written.*"

We often have what I call our *Sidebars*. Many times, he gave us additional information for a chapter. Therefore, I have created a section at the back of the book that would include those remarks, for they hold even more clarification. I even have what he says about the cross as we discussed the cross on the front cover of this book.

We have a saying in America: *This is going to knock your socks off!* Well get ready to pick up your socks, for the following chapters will stretch you, intrigue you, and play havoc with your belief systems. And you thought you had it all figured out (*smile*)! And so did we, but . . .

Here it is 2013 and Jeshua (who has now integrated with his higher soul, Sananda) had additional clarification he wished to make. Hence this revised edition!

Cynthia's Remarks: I am honored to be a part of this book with Chako and Jeshua. However, when Chako approached me to do the project, I wanted to say NO at first. I had doubts about my writing and channeling abilities even though I have been a channel for 15 years and had published a book. It just goes to show you that no matter what one has or has not accomplished, there is still the human part that can creep in and raise havoc. My response to Chako was going to be to decline the offer, but suddenly my body went into chills. Energy more powerful than anything I had ever felt went up and down my spine. It was so strong that it was hard for me to talk. It may only have been a few seconds, but it felt like 5 minutes went by before the energy subsided.

When the energy did finally leave, I immediately replaced the word "NO" with a "YES." Now mind you, what made this even more powerful was the fact that Chako had approached me to do this project just before doing a group channeling with Jeshua. Because of the way it all played out, I had no doubt that it was Jeshua who had provided me with this strong confirmation so that I would not refuse.

I wish I could say this book has been easy for me, but it has pushed me and reshaped me in every avenue of my life. This book has challenged my own beliefs, especially around Satan and caused me to have many discussions with Jeshua. So many times I have wanted to quit this project. I actually begged Jeshua several times to let Chako finish the book, or better yet, bring in another person to work with her. Instead, Jeshua sent people to me who knew nothing about the book to tell me they had a message from the Christ. They would proceed to tell me these types of things:

1. *"Christ is standing behind you and is holding a manuscript. Do you know what that means?"* This was told to me from a man for whom I was doing a reading.

2. One day while getting a massage, I was told. *"Oh, Christ just came in and wants you to know that he is pleased that you are helping him get off the cross!"*

Then she asked me if I understood what that meant. I remind you, these people knew nothing about a book. Of course, Jeshua knew I was in such conflict around the book that I was thinking of quitting, so he sent in helpers to keep encouraging me.

When I read Chako's remarks about knocking your socks off, I had to laugh. I don't know if it will or will not knock your socks off, but I will tell you it knocked **my** socks off!

Now that the book and its rewrite are completed, I have come to realize another deep truth for myself that contributed to my difficulty. I still believed in duality among other things and did not realize just how deeply all of my beliefs ran.

There are so many blessings that have come to me because of this project. Most of the gifts will never be known, for they are private; I am a much better person due to Jeshua's prodding and it is my hope that in some way you will also benefit from these words in your unique way.

AUTHORS' DISCLAIMER: According to Jesus/Jeshua ben Joseph, all that has been said in this book, *JESUS, My Beloved Connection to Humanity and the Sea,* has been said in many different ways in current times, as well as in times of old. *However, the information was not said through me, the Christ, Cynthia, and Chako before—the Trinity Energy. I have woven these threads of teachings in such a way as to reach a particular grouping of souls. All this information is from the Universal Mind of All That Is and is available to you as you connect with this Flow. Therefore, there could be concepts or thoughts that you may have read through other writings—some may match what I say now and some may not. Listen to your own heart and guidance as you read my words, Beloveds.*

Jesus/Jeshua ben Joseph (2013)

(Authors' note: Heather, our editor, told us that we needed a short explanation as to why there are dates printed after some of the chapters and in the SIDEBARS. Those dates relate to the linear time

when various lectures were given. Cynthia had so many challenges with health issues that it took 2 years before we could submit the materials to the publisher. Now we have added 2013 here and there so you will know where the revisions occurred.)

PROLOGUE

Jesus/Jeshua: It is at my request that I desire this book be written. I asked two very special Channels, Chako and Cynthia, to help me accomplish this goal. Through the union of the three, a power has been created that represents the authority of the tri-fold flame that is found within the heart. The tri-fold flame is your connection to the Father/Mother Creator.

When this authority becomes activated, it brings love and power into balance. This power affects all of creation. The two women whom I asked to bring this record forth were my sisters in my lifetime known as Jesus/Yeshua. However, our connection goes back to a long time before this world came into being. They are part of the flame found within the Father/Mother Heart. I had promised them when I walked as the Christ in the last days that they would be able to assist in bringing forth a different aspect of truth—a truth that would bring about peace and understanding in the hearts of humanity.

There are many ways and views that help construct a truth, and just as many ways of approaching it. Just like a compass that has the north, south, east, and west, all these positions make up the compass. Without these various directions, you would not have a workable method to help you find your way. No matter what your truth is, it cannot help but in the end guide you back to the only truth that has ever been viable: you are loved and you **are** love.

I am not asking you to give up your reality as you see it, but I am asking that you read my words and feel them with your heart. See if there is anything here for you that would help you to understand what this journey has been all about.

I would like to explain the meaning of the book cover. The ocean always has been a great love of mine. Many of my miracles were done around water. The cross represents two points of Light that intersect. At the place where they interconnect, creation occurs and life begins.

The dolphins are the guardians that have been assisting these points of Light since the beginning of time. They are all our friends. The dolphin upon the cross signifies life.

Finally, the words, the way I speak throughout this book, are as a brother and a friend. I purposely have chosen this type of language-ing, for it is time to focus on the beauty that is you and once-and-for-all not place me in such a high position that you feel that you will never be able to achieve my standing.

I remind you of the scripture *John 14: Most assuredly I say unto you, he who believes in me, the works that I do he will do also. And greater works than these he will do because I go unto my Father.* I went unto my Father so that I might prepare a place for you. The place that was prepared was your connection to your own Higher-Self so that once-and-for-all you could exit the human creation of ego and pain and return to your own sacred heart, the tri-fold flame and the reunion with Father/Mother Creator. This is where the greater works begin that are spoken of in the scriptures.

I capitalize the G in God, referring to you in your God state, not out of disrespect for Father/Mother Creator, but for respect for you in order to make a point of who you are in your true form.

These are my words, my Beloveds. Hear them with your heart; experience them with your soul.

Your friend, Jesus—a man who attained his own atonement, which is at-one-ment as a Divine Human.

(12-05-10)

(Authors' note: Jeshua requested that we change the word, "Reader" to "Beloveds," for the former keeps the person in his/her head; the latter keeps the person in his/her heart.)

INTRODUCTION

Jesus/Jeshua ben Joseph

I AM Jesus/Jeshua ben Joseph and this is my story.

This book is being written in such a way, that it will bring a little more of my personal story to light. It is also my desire that the teachings of 2,000 years ago be brought forward so that they can be easily applied and embodied in your current reality. Humanity has known me as Jesus/Yeshua ben Joseph. That has been my most famous lifetime. However, there is much more to me than what humanity has known. Many of the secrets about Earth and me have been pushed to the back and covered up—much like the saying *"swept under the carpet."* You have lost your remembrance. **This book is meant to trigger your memories. The energy of the book will help to awaken you**. I will be sharing with you more about myself and my life. I hope that you will begin to understand why I have such a great love for humanity, as well as for the sea. It is also my desire that through these two mediums, I will be able to bring forth a Light within every one of you so that you can lay down your fears and judgments and be the Light that you truly are and have always been.

There will be parts within this book that will be difficult for you, the reader, if you come from a strict Christian background, for it will not fit your beliefs of how you have thought of me. Your training (entrainments) of thinking in a particular way has contributed to the illusion that has caused you to forget the bigger truth. Through this book, it is my intention to set you free so you can own more of who you are and finally take me off the pedestal. I want you to be unfettered from the restraints that mass consciousness has created. The next cycle for the Earth is all about freedom, 2012 and beyond. When you break out of the mass-consciousness belief system, you will become unobstructed and then will be able to see the truth. It is all about you and freedom. That is why I have chosen to have this book written and even revised now (2013).

I will begin with an understanding of how to read this book, how to journey through it and create a reference point to come back to when you feel like there is no way what I am saying could be true. It's important that one look at all views of any experience with objectivity. You cannot have objectivity if you only view a subject matter from one angle or opinion.

To make this point clearer, I am going to give you an example of what I mean. I will use a chair. Think of a chair in your own mind right now . . . Visualize what I am about to say, but try to stay out of the box of how you first visualized the chair I told you to think about. I am suggesting that even though you think you know what a chair looks like . . . do you really? Let go of your ideas of a chair and instead, see my idea of a chair. We will view the chair from different angles to make the point.

We now come to the first person who is describing the chair and listen to what he has to say about what he is seeing: *what I see is a tall, stick-looking thing. It looks very solid; it is rounded at the top and it is square at the bottom. I see no space what-so-ever. It looks quite dark and it is made of what I would think might be a tree, but I am not certain. I can't see any place to sit so I don't believe this could possibly be a chair.*

The next observer moves to the left. This observer says *what I am looking at has a tall back. It also has flatness to it with a solid bottom that goes all the way to the floor. I see a hole, a dark hole on its side. It looks like there's an erosion of some sort. I cannot tell what it is. The rest of it has varying grains of different colors.*

The next person is standing in front of this object. He says *this looks like what I would call an L. It has a tall back, a very solid bottom to it and it is rounded in a way I have never seen before. I notice in the front that there are some rough places that are not totally smooth.*

The next person moves to the right and takes a look at it and says *oh, what I see is very different. I see a smoothness. It looks like whoever created this must have had a great deal of love for this because he has taken all of the edges and sanded them off. It is solid as well as smooth. I can also see some light color in it—it's very beautiful.*

The person above it looks down and says *I don't see any of that. All I can see is something sticking up and a flat surface. The flat surface looks like a table to me.*

The person underneath who looks up says *no, I do not see what any of you have seen. All I see is a round circle.*

Now the chair does not sound like any of the chairs you might be thinking of, but none-the-less, it is a chair. This is a chair I carved a long time ago in another lifetime. It was made out of a tree. Therefore, it does not have the legs that you would think of a chair having today. However, it still is a chair carved from a tree stump.

So can you see my point in doing this exercise? There are many different aspects (truths) of every story that is being told here on the Earth about me and all the other subjects that will be covered in this book. Every truth has its side of the story. All truths create a more complete picture. You do not have to throw out your other truths if you don't want to. I only ask you to try on yet another part to this story called PLANET EARTH and Jeshua ben Joseph's part in it.

The Sufis have a similar exercise that is used to help you understand the many different truths that are often presented. Instead of a chair they use an elephant. The person who is holding onto the trunk says *this is an elephant*. The person holding the tail says *that is not the elephant; this is the elephant*. The person holding a leg says *all of you are incorrect. This is the elephant*. And when in truth, it is all the elephant. Just like in truth, the chair is truly a chair no matter what your preconceived ideas were of what you had previously thought a chair should look like.

And so it is with my own story. The story I wish to reveal is about me, not necessarily the Yeshua ben Joseph you have heard about, although those are truths that are me, but I speak of **an aspect of me** not talked about. It does not take away from the Christ lifetime. I wish to add Light to that idea. However, I also wish to speak about many other experiences. Again I state that my desire in telling this story in this way is so you will now remove me from the pedestal and allow me to live in your hearts. We have all had experiences, and I have come to share intimately my own. The various stories I will share are being told so that you will have new, current-day teachings in a much simpler language that fit your present times. It is also my hope to paint an overview of many varying subjects in hopes it will encourage you to study them on your own. There is much to learn, my Beloveds. The Kingdom of God is Intelligence . . . not the ego/mind, but Intelligence.

I AM Jesus/Jeshua ben Joseph, your brother.

(Cynthia's note: The dictionary says that "intelligence is the ability to acquire knowledge by means of thought and reason." We often think just in terms of the Earth {physicality} and that kind of knowledge/intelligence. However, there is also other ways to acquire

knowledge/intelligence, like through obtaining information from that which has been kept hidden. These are the teachings that come from within when you touch-in and talk with God or Jeshua. Jeshua often talks to me about the Ladder of Life, as in Jacobs's ladder. As you obtain knowledge here on the Earth, it helps strengthen your mind as a container in which to hold the more profound Teachings of the Father. Father is pure Intelligence from what I have learned, and every question has an answer so that which has been termed "secret" is no longer hidden. I think this is what Jeshua is referring to. 2013)

1

YE ARE GODS

Do you know who God is? Is there more than one God? What would you say, my brothers and sisters, if I told you that the truth is that humanity is actually afraid of God and has done numerous things to separate itself from this Divine and loving Being? I would like to explore the deeper reasons most of humanity is afraid of God, as well as answer the opening questions. However, first let's start with some general understandings of who God is.

God, our Father/Mother, is present in every thing. God is loving, non-judgmental and filled with love for all of creation, and therefore, is unable to take sides and remains neutral in all things that occur in the Universe. You have heard this said many times and in various different ways: God is in the trees, mountains, birds, all things seen and unseen. God is in you, me and even in the creations made by man. Nothing exists that does not have the breath of God in it. Hearing the words and grasping this type of immense energy can be difficult and confusing.

God (Father/Mother) is both male and female and **is** and will always be the ultimate Creator. However, there are other Gods that create on behalf of and through using the energy of the Father/Mother. I will be referring to these inventors as Creator-Gods to help distinguish the difference. These Creator-Gods were born from the flame of the Father/Mother's heart. They were not born in the way a baby is born on the Earth but instead came from the heart energy of God, which is total love. God's energy is what makes up everything in the Universe, including the Creator-Gods. You existed in the Heavens before you came to Earth. You had a body that was made from this formless energy of the Father/Mother. Yes, **you** are one of the Creator-Gods that I am speaking about.

As I move through this chapter, I will be focusing more upon you, the Creator-God, than Father/Mother. The more understanding you gain of who you are and who I am, the easier it will be for you to return to your true God state. Many things have been forgotten in your time away from Heaven. **My** journey and desire was to show you through example the things that were possible for you, if you followed the teachings of the Father. It is a lonely place to live on a pedestal, my brothers and sisters, and I ask you to consider removing me from this position as you move through the book and gain more understanding about who you are.

My own abilities to perform miracles came from Father/Mother, and I have referred to this before in other works: *I of myself can do nothing, but with the Father who works through me, all things are made possible.* You and I possess the same abilities if you will only allow God's energy and love to flow through you once again. This energy is what connects you back to your Creator-God-Self.

Rules and regulations have been made upon the Earth to convince you that you are unworthy. Humanity believed a story that was created by human Beings in their own state of forgetfulness so they could have control. Believing any story that tells you something other than you are LOVE is to believe in falsenesses. In none of my teachings, my Beloveds, have I made reference to you as not being loveable or loved by God.

I would like to make up a very simple story about Creation and the part you played as a Creator-God to help you understand this journey. It is my hope this will shed some Light on the idea that *you are God.*

The Cosmos is made up of many different experiences. Remember, everything is Creator energy; there is always something new being brought into form through the intent of the Creator-Gods—the Beings I am speaking about are you and me. One day a group of Creator-Gods got together—remember we are not talking about a physical form; we are talking about an energy form of God. They wanted to create something that had never been done. Here is an example of what this might have sounded like if you were listening in on the conversation. It's not quite how it happened; however, it makes my point. One Creator-God said to the other Creator-God, *what can we do to add some spice to this eternal existence? We have created numerous planets and universes (energy used from Father/Mother) and this is getting very boring and tiring. I want to know myself differently and experience what I have created instead of just creating. What could be done that will not only deepen our connection to ourselves but will serve the universal energy (which is Father beyond our Father/Mother, but I will not address that right now) as well?* This is when a plan was devised to create a world and life forms to inhabit the Creation. Are you wondering what made this formation so different from other Creations that had come before? It's very simple. These life forms would have aspects of the Creator-Gods projected into them, and **they would be given free will**.

The Creator-Gods received all of the necessary approvals from the other Gods. (Remember; even though you are a Creator-God, there are still laws that exist in the Universe to ensure the safety of other formations.) Once everything was approved, the Creator-Gods began to make a planet. This was done through using intent and Father/Mother's energy, for this energy is in everything.

I will use another example to make this point a little clearer. For a moment, let's pretend that you are holding a jar of liquid that you can make bubbles from. All you have to do is pull out the stick and

3

blow, using your breath. The bubble you are blowing is similar to the Breath of God used to make planet Earth. So in this case you are the person who is the Creator of the bubble. You did not create the liquid, but you did create the bubble by **using** the liquid. Without you, the bubble would not exist and without the liquid you could not have made the bubble. This is how it works with Father/Mother and the Creator-Gods. Of course this is an over simplified version of the creation and there is a lot more to it than this, but for now it helps you to see how this happened.

So once the Earth was established, another Creator-God (female energy) took on the work of holding structure—molecules—together. She is called by many names, the most familiar being *Mother Earth* or *Gaia*. Once this was done, it was time for the Creator-Gods to place a pinch of themselves into the human form. It was known that giving free will to the human species could be very tricky and had to be monitored closely. Time was needed to allow this part of the self to learn how to use its power appropriately.

So the Creator-Gods waited and watched for a very long period of time for this new self to develop. This took many lifetimes. The Creator-Gods knew that if too much power was placed too quickly into their Earth aspects, there could be **a misuse of power**. This **would threaten the Universe and even destroy it**. So a plan was devised to take it very slowly, and volunteers like Angels and Guides agreed to help out in the unseen realms.

These Angels and Guides are also Creator-Gods. Never had a God given to another part of It-Self the ability to have this type of freedom to choose. The Creator-Gods knew they had no control over the Earth-selves because they had gifted them with free will. The only thing the God-Selves could do is to withdraw their support if their Earth-self had gotten too far off course.

The Creator-Gods were excited about this plan. They would finally get to experience themselves in a very different way. Having a physical body allows for certain sensations to occur that cannot be felt or experienced when one is in an energy-form. It was hoped that as the Earth-self matured and grew in its mastery that more of the Creator-God-Self would be able to merge into it. At some point, they would become One again, except this time it would be in a physical form rather than in the energy-form only. This would allow for many new experiences to occur and actually would change the Heavens forever. The total extent of where this would go was not known; however, the possibilities were endless. Up until this point, only Creator-Gods had had free will.

The way the Creator-Gods have experienced their Earth-selves while waiting for them to mature and master their ego is much like watching a movie. The movie is projected upon a screen, and the story of the movie is then reflected back to the person watching it. So this aspect of yourself was watching **you** having the experience!

Now let's create a little more passion and excitement for the movie by putting on 3D glasses. The movie you have been watching suddenly takes on a very different feel with these glasses—instead of watching the movie, you are actually experiencing it. You have begun to live inside the movie. There is a scene of a car accident and the person driving the car is badly injured. As you begin to merge with the movie, you at first only see the car accident without feeling it. Then the further you merge with it, you feel the car accident in your body, but you are not suffering. Then the deeper you merge with the movie, you begin to feel **and** suffer the effects of the car accident. You have totally forgotten it's only a movie, an illusion.

Deep inside there is a part of you that knows the movie is not true, but you are so caught up into the emotions that you can't remember what the truth really is. And for some of you right now, you don't want to remember. Perhaps you even think that you are unworthy and can't have something different. Your God-Self has now lost contact with you, the human-self, within its own creation. It's getting to see what you are experiencing, but it no longer can get your attention in order for you to wake up and realize it is all illusion.

Initially, this did not happen and all was going well with the plan; the part of you watching the movie and the part of you still in the Higher Realms were in full contact. However, as you began to get lost in the illusion (of the movie) you took on all of the pain, doubt, and fear you were watching and began to destroy yourself through your beliefs and thoughts. You turned away from the very thing that could save you. You were lost and your God-Self could not connect to give you the pass-code to awaken. It's like you were on the phone and suddenly you hung up on yourself—a disconnect!

A discussion occurred in the Heavens about the idea of pulling everyone's Earth-self out of the illusion and rejoining it with the Creator-God-Self. However, after much talking, it was decided that this would be too dangerous, not only for the human aspect, but for the other Gods and Their Creations in the Universe. No one knew for sure with free will what the abrupt merging of the two parts would create. Remember, one part lacked the knowledge that it was love and the other knew it was pure love—polar opposites ensued.

The God-Selves knew if a plan could not be devised, this aspect of them would be lost, perhaps forever, into the illusion. Many discussions occurred over eons of time about how to correct the condition upon the Earth. It was finally decided that the Creator-Gods had to wait until you, in physicality, decided through your own free will that you wanted to experience life differently. Great Teachers came and went in an attempt to show you how to awaken from this illusion. Through turning yourself over to the Greater Will, you finally will begin to see the truth of all things. Sooner or later everyone will make the choice to awaken. It's just a matter, of how long you want to suffer, my Beloveds.

In order to begin the process of awakening, start by accepting and forgiving yourself for believing that the movie was real. Through joining with your Creator-God-Self, you allow the flow of Father/Mother's love to enter you once again. Prayer is an excellent way to begin the process. Don't worry about the words or what you think you need to be saying; just start speaking what's in your heart. The Kingdom of Heaven will once again open to you. Here is a sample prayer—one you may wish to use:

> My *beloved Father/Mother, I am ready to awaken; teach me, and help me to see the truth of who I am. Help me to discover and to feel within myself the love that is all encompassing. Let me fully connect with all that I AM. Show me what I have been afraid to see. Do this with ease and Grace so that I might once again join my heart with yours. Open the doors so that I may walk as I was meant to walk. Thank You! Amen.*

Everything has a cycle to it. When you live upon the Earth, you tend to think more in terms of years or perhaps seasons, rather than in cycles. The **Heavens work in cycles of events**. The last 2,000 years was the Cycle of Christianity. My mission upon the Earth had many components to it—one of which was to challenge those of the **church** who said they were teaching Father's words. Instead, they **were serving the ego-self**. Their hearts had become hardened, which resulted in the darkest of all times for the planet. Through the fulfillment of my mission, humanity's heart began to open once again, and the way was prepared for this next Cycle of Freedom to occur.

I was not the only one working to wake humanity up from their 3D experience of the movie. Great Teachers came before me in hopes that humanity would awaken. However, when they did not awaken as planned, I began my preparation to come in and deliver the Teachings of the Father as Jesus. If it had not been for Pontius Pilot and the records that were written, little would have been known about me. I would have completed my mission and departed. The stories surrounding that time period would have been very different. It was the Father's Teachings that I came to impress upon man's heart, not me as the man.

Let's go back to the analogy of the movie theater. Would you agree that in order for a movie theater to operate and run effectively, there needs to be quite a few people involved? They don't get to watch the show because they must attend to their duties. If they were to get involved in the movie, no one would be there to make sure everything ran correctly. This is how I worked when I came in.

When I came in, I did so without personal karma. This is what allowed me to stay out of the drama that was playing on the movie screen. In other words, I never put on 3D glasses. Because of this, I saw and understood things very differently. I was like an usher and my job was to help humanity **leave** the theater. Now with that being said, I will return to the subject of cycles.

In 2012, a new cycle begins. This cycle will deal with your soul being set free from the bondage of believing that the movie you have been watching is real. When you join with All That Is and no longer see yourself as separate, you have joined with the Self that **is** a Creator-God. You now have the ability to create as a God while having a form. This is very important, because until now, that had not been available.

At the ending of 2012 there will be many cycles that will come to a close all at the same time. In the history of the Earth, you have never had so many cycles concluding all at once. You can view these cycles and their endings like that of the grand finale on the fourth of July.

Another way I can say this is when time-lines fold in upon one another coming at the end of a cycle, this can be likened to numerous waves hitting a shoreline during a turbulent storm—all at once. You can't do anything but watch as things are washed away. The washing process is making room for the new to be built again—a new dream. This is what will start happening on Dec. 21, 2012, and beyond. This is the beginning of the storm where the door way opens but the storm continues for some time, washing away all that will not fit the new dream. For the new vision is that of *Freedom.*

The world is not coming to an end, however a new and exciting journey begins for humanity. **Weather patterns** as well as **earthquakes will occur**. These changes can produce fear if you do not understand what is happening and why. There are many upon the planet who would want to capitalize on this fear and create chaos for humanity. I tell you, my brothers and sisters, do not buy into that fear, for it will only produce more—like attracts like. If you stay within your hearts of love you will be safe. Remember it is not the Father's desire for you to be harmed. Mother Earth also desires for you to be safe. Listen to that still, small voice within and it will guide you through these times of uncertainty. Remember, like attracts like. If you are in fear, you will bring fear to you. If you are in a place of love, only love can come to you. These are the Laws of the Universe.

The years 2000-2012 have been a period of time called *no-time.* You were in the hallway-of-life, moving from one room of experience to the next. You were waiting for the next doorway to open so you could begin your new life. Some people have described it as a feeling of being lost and not belonging. This period of no-time has given humanity the opportunity to shift perspectives from the old to the new—giving the new you the time you needed to figure out what you wanted to create in this new reality of 2013 and beyond. Most of this was being done on levels you were not even aware of. It is through the closing of the current cycle, that humanity will be catapulted into a new experience of what it means to be a Creator-God.

Even if you are reading this book after 2012, it is not too late to start reviewing your life and taking stock of what is and is not working for you. Ask yourself *what is really important to me?* Have you become so busy with the must have and have not's that you no longer know yourself? The confusion the cycles are producing in the hearts of humanity is so people can reassess themselves and their lives.

Be careful not to go into blame, shame, and guilt.* This will not get you where you want to go and only will create another side road, my Beloveds. Instead, honestly ask yourself simple questions like: *What are my values? Am I really happy? If not, why? What steps do I need to take to bring about an adjustment? Who do I need to make amends with but have been too stubborn to do so?* Pride is not your ally, my Beloveds. Be willing to take an honest and loving look at yourself and decide what you need to do in order to bring yourself back into alignment with the Father. True happiness can only come when you are fully connected with this loving energy. To think otherwise is a false belief.

There are **three gateways** for humanity: the first one being that of **2012.** Not everyone will choose this doorway because he or she is not ready. Do not worry, my Beloveds, about missing this door because there are two more portals through which you can go through—**2017** and around **2030**. This is not locked in stone. These doorways provide an opportunity for you to live in a higher vibrating realm and out of the drama. The higher you go in vibrations, the less chaos and pain you will experience. These higher vibrations allow you more connection to your Creator-God-Self. The Creator-Gods cannot and will not join you in the 3D theater (2013).

Paradigm changes can begin long before the dates listed. I remind you that these are approximate time periods for everything to occur, so allow for flexibility. An example of this is what happened on October 28, 2011, and 11-11-11. Some of what was scheduled for 2012 occurred during the October 28 and the 11-11-11 gateway. The remainder followed in 2012. All of the openings will be accompanied by smaller shifts in between.

Everything that happened to me when I journeyed upon the Earth happened in the best way possible to serve the needs of those present at the time. There is nothing for anyone to grieve about or to carry pain for around my death. If you continue to grieve, you keep the pain alive for humanity and this separates me from you. I ask you instead, to replace that grief with love and a desire to live and to help your brothers and sisters to awaken. Nurture yourself and commit to your own connection with your true Self. This would honor me more than my watching you lifetime after lifetime live in pain and grief. I showed you that life is eternal and what love looks like. Let that be the gift you remember from me and let that be the gift you now give to yourself.

My death allowed me to become Christed. Christ is a Principle through which one has gained all the necessary information needed to connect with his or her Creator-God-Self. For me, I became anointed with the blessing of knowledge from the Father. As I achieved this for myself, I was able to show you and pass this on to you, so that you too might become Christed.

As you prepare yourself to walk through the doorway that is fast approaching, no matter which one it is you choose, you will be moving into the higher vibrations and your own ascent into Christedness. **Your Christ Self is the midline between Heaven and Earth**. I will be there as your brother, welcoming you back.

I end this chapter bringing you back to my Introduction piece. There are many ways to walk around a chair and view it. My desire is to have you accept me as your brother and help me get off the cross humanity has placed me on. **I died not for your sins, as humanity has wanted you to believe, but instead, so you could wake up and see that I lived on after my death, as you will too.** I came so you could see the love of God moving through me and experience that and remember. What is sin anyway, my Beloveds? The **only sin** you have ever committed **was to forget you are love**. There can be nothing else, for everything that you have believed in or thought you did that was so sinful was an illusion. As each of you awakens, the movie you believed in disappears; so you see, sin does not exist. Let the guilt, blame and shame around the word go and realize you are love and a powerful Creator. Let us connect as a brother and sister once again and free you and me from the beliefs of separateness. It is time to quit denying that **you** are as great as I am. Let us become as One. Say daily and remember who you are:

I AM THAT I AM;

I AM PERFECTION; I AM ALL THAT IS; I AM GOD; I AM LOVE; EVERYDAY AND IN EVERY WAY MY LIFE IS REFLECTING THE PERFECTION THAT I AM.

I AM Jesus/Jeshua ben Joseph—brother.

John 13: 34-35 *A new commandment I give unto you, That ye love one another; as I have loved you, that ye also love one another. (34) By this shall all men know that ye are my disciples, if ye have love to another. (35)*

(*Chako: guilt seems to travel with **blame** *and* **shame.** *When one is present, the other two are lurking, waiting to be recognized. I call them* **The Triplets.** *One needs to address all three when one is processing inner work.)*

2

TREASURE CHEST

My brothers and sisters, buried within you are the treasures of the Universe. You contain the answers for mankind, as well as the advancement of Heaven. Through the experience of being human, you unleash the creation and ability necessary to form the new human Being that I refer to as a human God. It is the journey within which allows you full access to all of the knowledge and truths of the cosmos. Yes, it is all there inside the treasure chest of your own Being-ness. You may wonder how this can be. When you seek to know the truth with an honest and sincere heart, all must be revealed. Father/Mother has said the eternal flame of his/her heart will connect with the flame of the human heart and thus the new human will come into being. This creation will bring forth a change for everyone in Heaven, one that will create many new experiences.

Your life's journey is a rare and precious gift in which many in the Universe now want to partake. This was not always how it was; in the beginning there were those who thought this plan was destined to fail. There were numerous in-depth discussions amongst the Creator-Gods about the proposed idea. Countless talks took place around what could occur when humankind was given free will. Ultimately, it was agreed upon by all the Creator-Gods that the plan would proceed as long as safety measures were put into place. Levels of protection were designed to keep safe the other formations created by the Creator-Gods.

Currently, the events upon the Earth are chaotic and it appears like everything is out of order. However, underneath this chaos, there are many who are beginning the reunification process of bringing their two halves (Creator-God and human-self) back together. You are providing yourself with a very valuable experience to be present for your own evolution along with that of Mother Earth's. You are now becoming a new type of Being—a Human-God. It has taken millions of years for this evolution to reach this state of readiness.

Many have come from other Universes to view this remarkable event. Now everyone wants to come; however, currently there is *no room left at the inn,* so to speak. They will have to wait; for how long is not yet determined before this opportunity will be allowed for these Creator-Gods to try their hand with this type of creation. You, my brothers and sisters, are the ones who are rewriting the Heavenly realms.

The masses began their awakening starting in the 1930s. Little bits at a time, more and more people have awakened to the idea that there is something more out there. In less than 100 years, look at how quickly you have evolved and realized that you are more than you have thought yourselves to be. What you have accomplished in the last 100 years, as great as it has been, is nothing compared to what is coming. The school called *Planet Earth* is a great success and will soon be re-opened, in the distant future, for enrollment. (A little humor here from your brother.) I ask you, my brothers and sisters, to celebrate who you are!

John 17:5 And *now, O Father, glorify thou me with thine own self with the glory which I had with thee before the world was.*

This is what was meant when I spoke the words *glorify me with thy glory*. The knowledge that I am sharing with you is so you too might receive the same glory—that of the Father—the glory that is rightfully yours before you came into this world—the reunion of you, your Creator-God-Self with Father/Mother.

Let's explore more about the purpose of having a human body to experience life through. Remember, after all, the Creator-Gods felt this body was invaluable for the growth of their/your souls. When you can't remember who and what you are, you must find your way through exploring the many paths found within. This type of journey is very different from the one that knows what the outcome will be around each corner. So it is with the human-self and the Creator-God-Self. Each is a valuable path; however, the journey within brings forth knowledge in a very different way.

I would like to provide you with an experience to help you better understand my words, a journey that will perhaps take you deeper into your own soul. Have you ever followed a path out in the wilderness that you had no idea where it would take you? The very act of not knowing keeps the excitement alive, and everything you encounter brings forth feelings of enthusiasm and wonderment. Let us start our journey coming upon a grouping of trees. As you get closer and closer, you are able to see how thick this clump of trees actually is and upon closer observation it looks more like a forest than a group of isolated trees. There seems to be some sort of path in front of you. The markings on the path are not totally clear; however, with discernment you think you can make your way deeper into the forest and explore what is there.

You notice the forest floor is covered with newly fallen leaves of various shades and colors. Each step you take reminds you of the sounds of a crackling campfire. The smell in the air is clear and crisp with a hint of dampness to it. The temperature is delightful, not too cold or too hot for an early morning walk. There is a slight fog-like mist hanging high up in the forest's canopy. The woods provide various shades of colors reminding you of an artist's pallet. You never knew there could be so many shades of green. Some of the greens are rich and velvety while others have a tinge of yellow and orange beginning to appear around the outer edges; yet some are bleeding entirely into the green leaf consuming its original color. The sight is soothing to your eyes; you can't help but feast upon all of the vibrant colors.

You can hear hundreds of different kinds of birds talking in the trees tops. They have their own life—way up there. Your mind wonders off as you continue walking along the small and barely visible path. You can't help but think what it might be like to live up in the canopy. Suddenly, you notice something in the trees in front of you. As you approach, there are some inspiring spider webs hanging in amongst a cluster of trees.

Some of the spiders have woven their webs out in the open, between the tall trees, creating quite an impressive sight. Some of the webs are nearly three feet tall and almost that same size, if not a tad bit bigger, in width. The web is held on each side through the support of each tree. You ponder to yourself how wise these spiders are to use the trees to provide such strength for their impressive nettings. A hint of light peaks through the canopy above, providing the right amount of light that creates the perfect stage lighting, showing off the morning dew on the numerous webs that are displayed. *What an impressive piece of forest art,* you think to yourself. Time stands still. You continue to wander through the various pieces of spun-art, some of which were being created right before your very eyes. You are not even aware that time had stopped until you suddenly hear the sounds of the forest once again. This jolts you back into present reality and out of your hypnotic state. You realize you must get moving along. However, you find it hard to tear yourself away from this spectacular show of creative art. It takes a bit of doing, but finally you force yourself to step back upon the path.

After walking along for some time, you note the numerous vines as they journey first up one tree and then down the other, reminding you of some old movie you had seen. You envision yourself swinging upon some of the vines. The forest has changed its colors as you walk deeper into it. You marvel at how much you love nature and its natural raw beauty. Everything feels so new and full of vibrancy that you never want to leave. Suddenly, you hear a loud sound on your right. As you turn, you see what looks like a mother deer and her baby standing there watching you. As your eyes meet, it feels as though each of you totally understand everything there is about one another.

There is no fear for either of you, but instead there is a quiet unspoken understanding of safety as well as an immense love. It feels all peaceful and warm inside you. You think to yourself that this must be the way God loves—totally and without reservation. Then as quickly as they appeared, they disappear into the forest.

My Beloveds, I will stop the story here and leave you with these questions to ponder:

1. What kind of experience would you have had if you knew everything there was to know about the forest? You knew beforehand the feeling of the forest; you knew you would see the spider webs and you knew you would meet the family of deer. Everything was known before you entered the forest because you created it. So would your experience have been as joyful as **not** knowing?

2. If you wanted to experience something differently, how would you design your creation? The Creator-Gods knew

they could not experience their creations in the same way you experienced the forest unless there was something done differently. So it was designed that you would not know everything!

The Earth is a school where one has experiences called *lessons*. Some of these lessons are pleasant and some are not, but each one teaches you what you do and do not want in your life. The knowledge gleaned through this process helps you learn about power, love, pain, sorrow, and happiness. It is through your physical form that you are able to experience life in a way that could never have happened otherwise.

The indigenous cultures understand that the lessons in life are actually blessings. There are even some who at the close of each year choose not to give gifts but instead share their blessings of growth with one another. If you could view your life's schooling as a precious treasure of understanding, one that is allowing you the ability to better understand yourself/life, you would become filled with a lot more joy and peacefulness.

I encourage you to ask yourself next time you are met with challenges, *what are the gifts that I am receiving from this experience?* The more you take accountability for your life as the creator, the more you will understand the purpose. One perspective will chain you to the illusion (victimhood); the other one will provide freedom. Thus, you will be seeing life through God's eyes, which have become your own eyes, and then life really begins.

Your body is made up of more than just elements like oxygen, carbon, hydrogen etc. These elements alone are not capable of making a body like the human form work. Do you remember the statement upon the Earth, *Shhh, your body is hearing everything you are saying*? Well, my Beloveds, it is true; your physical form has its own intelligence and it hears everything. This intellect has been called by various names and here are just a few: *body divas, intellect,* and *elementals*. I would prefer to call them *elementals*. **You are not your body and your body is not you.** It is important to remember that these elementals have their own energies and operate separately from you and yet they are in partnership with you. This energy was summoned forth by the Creator-Gods in order to help you in your soul's journey here. These elementals lovingly volunteered to be of service to you.

Have you ever thought about how your autonomic nervous system just seems to know how to regulate your breath, digestion, heart rate, and perspiration? How does a baby's body regulate its temperature? What causes the infant to know how and when to stretch its arms and legs? How does it know how to crawl? **You** are not getting on the floor and crawling in front of the baby. Yet it seems to know how to do it all on its own. A baby does not know what food is and yet it knows when it's hungry. How can this be? After all, **you** did not teach the baby what hunger is.

When your spirit comes into the body, it does so with no knowledge about how to take care of itself. It has not been taught yet. **The body, from the moment of conception, is cared for by the elementals**. So it is with animals, for their bodies just seem to know what they need to do to live. They know they need to eat. Therefore, the baby will cry to get the attention of the mother to feed it. Watch a batch of newborn baby birds and how they cry when they are hungry. It is a beautiful sight and sound.

As growth and development begin to take place, more of your spirit begins to come on board—more of you take on the body after a while. However, the elementals never leave. They are always there helping you sustain the body.

The quality of your life can be improved as you work to gain more understanding about the elementals and work with them instead of against them. They agreed to help you on this journey of learning about being human. They wanted to be here to support you as you worked on the lessons you came to experience. In the process of learning about your human-ness, you often make choices that harm the body elementals. Damaging effects occur in the body around certain foods (*coffee*), strong drink (*alcohol*), cigarettes, and drugs. Yet the elementals continue to work to help keep the body as healthy as possible, even though you are abusing it. That is until there is too much mistreatment, and it can no longer hold at bay the inevitable disease and death sequence.

Through your desire to change how you experience your body, you will begin to create a partnership with the elementals. Seeing them more as helpers, you begin to work more in tandem, helping you to overcome disease, food addictions, etc. Their true mission is to help enhance your quality of life.

The elementals have been with you from lifetime to lifetime. They know what lessons you have and have not learned in conjunction with the body. Their agreement was to stay with you until you completed your sojourn here upon the Earth. A good metaphor of what I am saying would be the experience the channel (*Cynthia*) had. In a past life, she was in a male form and enjoyed strong drink to such an extent that it prevented her from accomplishing her mission.

In each life, you have things you are to do and learn in order for your soul to evolve. The body elementals allowed her to learn the lesson around alcohol in that lifetime, even though they themselves suffered and ultimately death occurred due to liver and kidney failure. In her present life when she tries strong drink, a violent reaction occurs within the body. The body elementals are protecting her from having to repeat this experience since the lesson was already learned.

All is done in conjunction with her Creator-God-Self. I remind you that the human part of her does not remember that she has learned this lesson, but her Creator-Self and the elementals do. So they protect her from going down that path again. However, with free will, she could ignore the sickness and drink anyway.*

The elementals are your friends, and through this union with them, you will be provided with one of the most intimate opportunities to learn about partnership and self-mastery. As you work on this partnership, in return you are granted good health. This partnership also provides you with the opportunity to transcend death, if you so choose.

There are already many alternative modalities currently being used to talk with the body elementals. Take body testing, for instance. The practitioner uses a technique to speak with the body and ask questions to help determine what is needed. Even though two people may have the same illness, the remedy may need to be changed. Each person has a different set of elementals, and therefore, each body can react very differently to the same treatment. Traditional medicine does not acknowledge this currently. This will not be so in the future, as more of you awaken. No one knows better what is needed for the body to heal than the elementals that have been taking care of it. When I walked the Earth, I healed the sick through what was called *miracles*. I tell you I knew the laws of how to communicate with the Higher-Self and Father/Mother. I also had the knowledge of the person's body elementals. I knew how to draw forth the flame of life held within that person. This is what did the healing.

I would like to give you another example to help you better understand the correlation of the body and its elementals. Let's pretend that a car and a human body have a lot in common. For the most part, a car is made up of metal and plastic. The human body is made up of water, oxygen, and carbon for the most part. Plastic and metal all by themselves cannot do much and are rather useless until a design and purpose is created. This is also true for the human body. A design and purpose must be created before you can do anything with water, oxygen, and carbon. Just because a car is molded and shaped into a beautiful vehicle, does that mean it is functional? Without an engine, the car is useless. The human body is much the same. Without its elementals, it cannot operate.

Let's explore the car a little further and see what else is needed. Can a car drive itself down the street? No, it requires a driver. Can a body fulfill its mission without its spirit? No, it will eventually die. What will happen if the driver forgets to change the oil and uses bad gas? Yes, eventually it will die. This is no different for you with your body. When a person is young, he/she can get by with things and the body seems to keep going, but eventually it breaks down and death is the outcome. This is not how it was meant to be.

Everything you do is a journey of self-discovery. There is a voice within you that is alive. You can talk with this Intelligence if you will take the time to connect. Don't ask it/them to heal you while you keep doing the very things that made you ill. Remember, this is a partnership.

An important part of being human, my Beloveds, is to understand the **ego**. Your ego can be of great assistance to you or it can lead you down a path of destruction. Up to this point, humanity has mostly followed it down the path of destruction. Ego is really not very difficult to understand when you begin to think of it as a friend with child-like mannerisms. **If you are not taking care of yourself, your ego-self will act out**. It will do whatever it needs in order to make you aware that it has been forgotten. This is what is at the root of jealousy, lying, or seeking approval from others.

However, if you are taking care of yourself and valuing **you**, ego will not act out. It has no need to. If it starts to raise its head, stop yourself, pay attention to you and what your needs are. Then work to meet your own needs. Do not try to take care of these needs by attempting to make or entice others to praise you or do something they don't want to do. If you take this route, you are going to dig yourself into a deeper hole and feel more unsatisfied than before you started. I tell you my Beloveds; there never is enough praise in the world to satisfy you. What is needed is for **you to feed yourself** that praise and love.

Let me provide you with an example of how to do this. Let's say your mate forgets your birthday. This seems to be a habit and year after year, there is no acknowledgement. As your birthday starts to approach, you start feeling agitated and angry. Then as the big B-day arrives and your worst fears are realized, there is a big fight because you become wounded that you were forgotten. Just because he or she forgot does not mean you are not loved.

You are the one who created the story in your head that they did not love you or they would have remembered. No, my Beloveds, this story is all about you. What you are trying to do is to get your **own** attention through ego acting out. It wants you to know that **you** forgot you. You were the one born, and it is your job to celebrate your own birth. Yes, my Beloveds, it is nice when you are acknowledged. However, it is even nicer that you do something special for yourself. You see, when you wait for another person to acknowledge you, that is the way of the human ego—that is the path of destruction. If anyone happens to remember you on your birthday, then consider it an extra blessing, but not a necessary one.

Ego will not act out when you are showing up for you. Ego will always act out when you are waiting or wanting someone else to do your work. If you consider ego your friend, then each time it acts out, you will begin to realize that it is only showing you that you have forgotten to take care of yourself through doing nurturing things for yourself. How many times do you try to manipulate others in an attempt to satisfy your needs? This is the destructive side of ego. Yet, I tell you that if you take care of your needs, self-accountability, then ego will not act out because it got what it wanted all along—love. And it got it from the person it wanted it from the most, **you!**

Let's go back to the example I gave of the mate forgetting you on your birthday. What is stopping you from throwing yourself a birthday party and inviting everyone you can think of? Whoever said that a birthday party needed to be thrown by someone who was not having the birthday? After all you were the one born; it is your day not theirs. So take charge, my Beloveds.

Only you can give to you the love that you need. This is what ego really wants you to realize. It desires for you to remember that a time long ago you loved and honored yourself totally. You would never entertain thoughts of lack or not being good enough. Ego's whole purpose is to get your attention that you went to sleep on the job of loving self. As soon as you get this, you will no longer have ego issues. And anytime ego does surface, all you have to do is ask yourself, *what is it I am in need of doing for myself?*

Let me propose some questions for you to ponder: What changes would occur in your life if you focused upon loving yourself in each moment? What would happen if you believed in yourself totally? Ah, the world as you know it would change instantly.

Your body has chakras, glands, and energy fields which provide a great deal of help to you, as you will soon see. The body is quite a remarkable gift. The word *chakra* means a type of vortex or wheel. These are spherical in nature and help direct power from the energy fields around you to the glands within the body so they can operate properly. There are seven major chakra centers in the physical body along with smaller ones. Think of them as doorways that distribute your life force throughout the body. These doors/pathways are vital for your development.

The art of balancing and maintaining your energy fields and chakras takes place as you learn mastery over your emotions. When this is accomplished, others no longer affect you, but instead, you affect them. In other words, those around you change to match **your** energy. Nothing is being taken from you. It's just that you begin, my Beloveds, to influence others for the better. **If you could look inside yourself during this stage of mastery, you would see your chakras appear bowed-out or convex**. This is what my chakras looked like when I walked the Earth as Jesus. This is why so many people healed just by being in my presence.

Most of humanity's chakras at this point on the Earth are concave (curved in). This means they take in the energy of those around them, whether it is positive or negative. Concave chakras are like a bowl that scoops up the energy put out by others and brings it back into the body. On an unconscious level, this is an attempt to fill yourself up. However, this will never work because **it is only through mastering yourself and drinking in the energy from the Creator-God and Father/Mother that the chakras can become convex**. Eventually, as humanity awakens into its own power, everyone's chakras will become convex.

At this stage of development, you will reach a mastery that allows you to bring forth all that you desire. All you must do is think a thought and it is yours. At this point of development, you no longer are capable of focusing on negative and harmful thoughts. My Beloveds, if you are feeling that this is too much for you to achieve, I tell you now it is not, for you are destined for this type of greatness.

Now let's briefly explore the glands within the body that are fed by the energy of the chakras. Glands are power points. These points allow you to receive urgings from Spirit (Creator-God-Self and Father/Mother). Through practice and meditating, you begin to connect. Meditation helps still the chatter of the mind. **When your mind is always running, you keep yourself disconnected**. You don't need hours, dear ones. Just doing five minutes twice daily can bring about results. Start with five minutes in the morning before starting your day. Cleanse and purify your mind and body by bringing in the golden white Light from your Creator-God-Self. See this Light moving through your entire body and into all your cells. Then sit quietly, allowing nothing to enter the mind and body except the feelings and frequencies of *love*. If you have difficulties visioning the Light, then call me forth to help you. See me standing in front of you pouring my love into you.

Then in the evening cleanse the mind from all the thoughts that you have entertained throughout the day. Your mind should be empty and clean before retiring for the evening. You will find this simple yet profound exercise a helpful tool in connecting you with your guidance.

Let's look at the gland called the *hypothalamus.* This gland provides a lifeline of pure energy to the autonomic nervous system and the endocrine system. It is through this gland that your life purpose is able to come into manifestation. The *pineal* gland connects you to the Higher-Mind of Father/Mother God. The *pituitary* gland is in charge of your sacred sight, which is located in the third eye. This allows you to see and know the unseen realms. Your *thyroid* governs the throat. This gland works directly in relationship with your **sacred heart** (access to it is through both shoulder blades in back) Sounds and vibrations from the Universe come through the throat (thyroid area). Your *kidneys* regulate the inward waters of life. You are mostly water in your makeup; therefore, it's through the kidneys that you are connected to the Cosmic oceans—Universal flow. This is why inharmonious energies are filtered through the body's kidneys so they can be cleansed and purified.

Your *adrenals* lend strength and power to you. They are sensitive to conflict, such as anger and jealousy, to name just a few. Your adrenals provide you with *endorphins* (happiness). This is the energy of which the New World will be created. Your *thymus* gland is the master communicator because it talks to every cell in the body. Through feeding these tissues/glands with this life—sustaining energy, healing occurs.

Your chakras and glands are connected to the energy fields. They are made of energy and produce channels of power that help run and maintain the various levels. These fields are called *subtle bodies* and intermingle with the physical body. These fields assist the body, mind, and soul in their progression back to Oneness. All of these parts of the body are maintained through the efforts of the elementals who are working on your behalf.

Up to this point, we have been speaking about the Higher-Aspect of you as a Creator-God. I would like to change the words I have been using for Creator-God to *I AM Presence* instead. The *I AM* term means you are All Things and you have come from the energy of All

That Is. Father/Mother created your I AM Presence with the energy of Their Heart. Your I AM called forth the creation of the human body through the use of this energy and then gave it purpose.

When you use the words *I AM*, the Presence is called in to act on your behalf. This action releases energy from Father/Mother Creator to your individualized I AM Presence, which resides in the Higher Energy Realms that we have been referring to as the Creator-Gods. The Presence then brings forth the actions of that request. This is why it is important not to use the words *I AM* unless it is something you really want to create. How many of you without thinking say, *I AM broke? I am Ill? I am tired?* You have just called forth the act of being this way and you did it through using the words *I AM*.

When *I AM* calls are put out, it brings a concentrated point of Light from your Presence because you requested it. So make sure you are ready to receive what it is you are calling forth.

Ahh, so now your thoughts are *I AM rich. I will be rich because I used the words I AM.* No, my beloved that is not how it works. How many I AMs have you said around *I AM broke*? What you have done is create a basket filled with the energy of being broke because you called it forth. A few *I AM rich* thoughts do not instantly undo what you have created. It does not happen that way.

Become hyper-diligent, my Beloveds, at the first signs of any thoughts that are not what you desire to create in your life. Make a call to your I AM Presence in my name, the Lord Jesus Christ, to help you with the negative thinking. Ask for the removal of such thoughts. Then replace it with those thoughts and feelings that you desire to create. Or you can use the following prayer:

My beloved I AM Presence, I summon you forth in the name of the Lord Jesus Christ. I ask for your assistance *along with the loving help of the Masters. Help me in purifying my mind of all negative thoughts. I ask that the violet flame cleanse and purify my mind and thoughts **now**. May I become flooded with the Golden Light of the Presence to help me in keeping my thoughts clean and clear of all negativity. Fill me up with only that which is uplifting for my spirit. I thank thee for your loving assistance. Amen*

My Beloveds, there are many thoughts that randomly enter and exit the mind in each moment. You cannot help what comes into the mind because you are a part of the human consciousness, but you can help how long a thought stays. Here is another prayer you may want to use to help you in mastering your thoughts:

Mighty I AM Presence, my beloved Father/Mother Creator, and the Ascended Masters, I call you forth in the name of the Lord Jesus Christ. I call upon the brilliance of your Divine Light and love to help illuminate my mind so I might become aware of my thoughts, actions, and deeds which have created blockages in my body. I ask that the violet flame blaze through my body, transmuting all discord and return me to a perfect state of health and well-being. Amen.

The use of the violet flame is a great gift brought forth to help mankind transmute negative energy. You can call upon it at any time. The violet energy is used in the Heavens, as well as on other planets for the transmuting of energy.**

The purpose of this chapter is to nudge you to see the gifts that you possess within. I have spoken through many different voices upon the Earth in an effort to help you remember the Teachings of the Father. Some of these voices used came through various religious orders and others have not. The voice I am using in this book is quite different. My mission now is to awaken you more to who you are and who I am so we can become as One. These are different times, and you are no longer bound by the laws of 2,000+ years ago. The essences of my Teachings remain the same; however, you are entering a time of freedom. Therefore, I use different wording and examples to teach the lessons of Father. Humanity will be taking its rightful place in my Father's House very soon. Heaven will be upon the Earth and enjoyed by all who are here.

Your lives are much like the example of the chair I carved. Each position viewed and the height from which it is viewed is bringing a different perspective. In the end, it is still a chair. In the end, all the Teachings are the same. Love yourself and love one another.

(*   Chako also had a past life as a wino. See SIDEBARS and read the Chapter 2 section.)

(** Saint Germain is the Keeper of the Violet Flame.)

3

HEAVENLY ASSISTANCE

*Until you find your own heart, you cannot change the
world. Until you understand your heart is everyone's
heart, you cannot change the world. When this is finally
understood, the world changes and Oneness begins.*
Jesus (Jeshua ben Joseph)

Now that you better comprehend who you really are and the gift of
your physical form, let us come to understand a few more of those
who lovingly share their energy of Light to support humanity in
its growth. The unspoken ones that I am referring to are the Great
Cosmic Beings who come from the Great Central Sun. These Beings
bring forth 12 rays of Light to help assist the Earth and humanity.
The rays contain a Goodness within them that comes from Father.
These are valuable gifts and help further mankind's growth and
development. The Earth is a school for mastery, designed for and by
the Gods—your I AM.

Today you refer to these Cosmic Beings by another name,
Astrological Signs. They are much more than a planet or a sign.
They are alive as you are alive. However, their bodies are comprised
of Light. There are cities of Light, in the Etheric realms, in various
areas all around the Earth. Each city has a different mission. There is
a portal over the Sierra Desert which the 12 Cosmic Rays use to step
down the intensity of their Light rays so that they can assist Mother
Earth and humanity. It is here that they are able to shift their Light ray

into a more compatible form before bringing it onto the planet. Each ray brings forth a Goodness that humanity can learn from. These gifts are the Assets of Father, my Beloveds. The ancient cultures had a different way of learning from the Cosmic Beings than you do today. People would go to a particular temple where they could connect with that Cosmic Being and receive the teachings from Father through these Beings of Light. This helped each individual move closer into his/her mastery. However, as mankind dropped deeper into the realms of density, the Temples of Light could no longer teach the lessons of the Father's Goodness in the same way. A new way needed to be devised—hence Astrology was created. This provided a way for the teachings to continue in the denser vibrating realms.

The lessons learned in each lifetime from the Astrological signs help bring forth the qualities needed so that you can achieve self-mastery. In time, you will bring all of the 12 virtues into full bloom within yourself. Once this is accomplished, mastery over the human part of yourself is accomplished, and you will once again become reunited with your I AM Presence. All 12 Cosmic Beings and the Goodness they bring forth come from the pure energy of Light and love from the Father/Mother Creator. However, how mankind receives this energy is based upon influences—one being the belief systems of the person. Another influence is the Earth's orbit and how the various energy patterns influence the sign. (2013) Let us take a look at the Sun sign *Virgo*. There are many gifts Virgo brings to the student while being under this influence. However, your own tendencies within the emotional body can influence and stir things up, making the virtue being offered not seem like a gift at all—for instead of balance, you are apt to go into extremism, oversensitivity, self-doubt, inadequacy, and avoidance. As you master yourself, you find that instead of extremism you now have moderation; instead of self-doubt you now have self-confidence; instead of avoidance you have order and so on. These Beings of Light make available to the receiver the gift of the Father's Goodness. However, it is up to the persons who receive it to use it in a way that will bring themselves back in touch with their authentic self.

I will speak now of Cynthia to make this point a little clearer. She has a Virgo moon. The sign of Virgo affects her emotions because it is her moon sign. If she does not master her emotions, then this leads to dis-ease in her emotional body. She chose to be born with this influence in this lifetime because she wanted to master the emotional body.

Without lessons, it would be difficult to tell if you are actually growing. As a human Being, you need something against which to measure yourself. Let's say you are a Virgo and you know that you have a tendency to doubt yourself. So, on an unconscious level, when the lesson is brought to you, you take that energy and create for yourself situations that produce more doubt. I ask you, does the Cosmic Being and the energy it brings create the issues in your life, or is it the way you have chosen to handle it that creates the difficulties? If you know you tend to have lots of self-doubt, yet you resist working on the issue and choose instead to ignore it, does it really go away? No, my Beloveds, it just keeps coming back to see you on another day, wearing a different set of clothes suited for the circumstances being presented.

Now, if you stay in resistance again and ignore it for the second time, the third time, and so on, you will begin to create a situation where you fall into victimhood. **Nothing can ever be solved from the level in which it was created**. It is through your willingness to become accountable that you begin to set yourself free from the chains that bind you. Remember the statement, *what you resist persists*. It's true, my Beloveds. The gift of all lessons is to surrender to the experience and learn the lesson presented and receive the Goodness of Father from that experience.

In each lifetime, you work through various aspects of the human ego and its reaction to a particular astrological sign. You have just been presented with the ability to unearth the Goodness that sign holds for you. You are not born under the same Sun sign lifetime after lifetime. However, you are still under a particular influence that a sign brings to you until it is learned. Every thirty or so days all of the aspects of the twelve houses that were once temples will influence you. Some are easier to pass through than others because of the lessons you have learned. The gift that life brings to you is that of discovery—the ability to experience yourself in a new and different way, as many times as you like. Through each reinvention, you will get to know yourself differently. This is one of the wonderful things about having more than one lifetime upon the Earth. You design each life for yourself and you change it slightly so you can experience yourself in a new way, all the while completing the lessons carried over from the previous life. Through learning how to work with the following attributes, you will obtain the mastery you seek and the gift of Father's Goodness. These gifts are present in every lesson you encounter: **Power** (*the right use of*); **Divine Will** (*the meaning of*); **Discernment** (*wisdom*); **Love** (*Divine*); **Purity** (*innocence*); **Hope** (anticipation of); **Devotion** (*to yourself and God*); **Faith** (that which is unseen); **Peace** (*tranquility*); **Charity** (*mercy*); **Patience** (tolerance) and **Compassion** (empathy).

You also have around your physical body fields of energy called *auras*. Your auras are directly connected with the chakra system spoken of in the previous chapter. Each level is present to help you in reconnecting the human aspect to your I AM Presence and the Father/Mother God. Your I AM is the one who helps to slow the energy down to create each auric field. These fields are built by a team of helpers, which include the elementals. The closer the fields come to the body the slower the vibration. The field closest to the body is referred to as the *lower etheric body* and is directly associated with the physical body.

The etheric body is like a blueprint of the physical body. When you have lifetimes after lifetimes of discord, you start stuffing this energy into your fields in an attempt to get away from it. Let me explain further. Right next to the lower etheric body, you have the etheric emotional body and next is the etheric mental body. **All three bodies can be called the *human personality*.** They interpenetrate one another and overlap into the physical body. The point I am making, my Beloveds, is that just because you die, these fields do not die with the physical body but stay instead in the inner realms until your next life. (I made reference to this when I spoke of the elementals holding your patterns from one lifetime to the next.) This is how the records that are pertinent for your stages of growth are stored from lifetime to lifetime. Intense feelings stored in these records (emotional body) are projected back to you (like a mirror) and will surface again (like a magnet) until you find ways of resolving the issue.

Here are some examples of things that can be stored from one lifetime to the next: **relationships, boundaries, illnesses, emotions, health, and personal use of your power.** So you can see if you have unresolved issues from another lifetime and you have wondered why things keep coming up again and again, this is why. As you move through your issues mirrored to you in your fields, you will find yourself reconnecting back to the God-Self. When I was delivering the Teachings of the Father 2,000+ years ago, **my**

Apostles represented—mirrored to humanity—**the 12 signs of the zodiac**. Even today the Teachings from their lives continue to influence humankind. I remind you that this was a time of great darkness for the Earth, and Teachings had to be done in ways that were not always so obvious and yet were able to be received through the unconscious levels.

(Side note here: Yes there were 13 Apostles and there are actually 13 Astrology Signs and more on that will be forth coming to humanity. However, I will not address that in this book as it is pre-mature for what I am attempting to achieve. 2013)

Let us speak of *Doubting Thomas*. How many of you have those doubting characteristics within yourself? No one who journeys upon the Earth has escaped this lesson of mastery. Then we have the opposite, *John the Beloved*, who held the attributes of *faith*, knowing within himself the truth of all things. Each soul chooses the sign to come in under that is best suited for his/her growth. The deciding factor for the soul is what will bring forth the greatest opportunity for advancement. My Beloveds, it matters not if you have 30 lifetimes as a Virgo and only 12 as a Sagittarius. What matters are the lessons and Goodness gleaned from each sign and how you embody them. If the main theme in your lifetimes has been around fear of not being successful, know that some signs will trigger this more than others. However, as you overcome this issue, then you will not experience it again no matter what sign you are born under. Enjoy the journey! *The Kingdom of God is within.*

Your beloved brother Jesus (Jeshua ben Joseph)

4

THE ENERGY OF DISCORD

My Beloveds, **discord is inharmonious energy** that has accumulated in such a way that it creates difficulty for the planet and humankind. **Discord is a slowly vibrating frequency**. This type of energy is created through anger, rage, negative thoughts, fear, blame, and jealousy. It is through these emotional feelings that actions like criticism of another, vengeful deeds, judgments, hurtful words, and war are acted out in the world. These, along with other thoughts and actions, are responsible for producing the inharmonious forces that are creating the problems you see in the world today. Let us take one of the words above and see how it might play out in everyday-life. Through this process you will come to understand how inharmonious feelings are being created in the world. The feeling-word we will be dealing with is one of *worthlessness*—**a self-worth issue ignited through the action of criticism**. For a moment, pretend that you are the person this is happening to. Let's say you are getting ready to go out for the evening and you have been feeling badly inside yourself. Life has dealt you some hard lessons recently. You have used food to console yourself during these difficult times; therefore, you have put on 15 extra pounds. This is more than you have ever weighed. It has been many months since you have gone out with your friends to just let loose and have a good time. This is your opportunity to do something nice for yourself. You put on one outfit after the other. Each change of clothing reflects to you the obvious; you have gained weight and no matter what you do, those extra pounds are not going

38

to go away. You are mentally giving yourself a beating for having gained so much weight.

Suddenly your friend rings the doorbell. She has arrived to pick you up. She does not know that you are feeling frustrated because your clothes won't fit. She only sees the outfit you have on when you answer the door. She does a quick up and down look at you and says, without realizing this will hurt you because you have always been bluntly honest with each other in the past: *That dress really makes you look fat. Have you gained weight? I don't remember it fitting you that tightly the last time you wore it.* You are crushed and immediately you inform her that you are not going out and that you want her to leave right now.

You feel humiliated and very emotional. You are thinking to yourself, *How could she be so unkind?* Of course, your friend is bewildered; she did not think she said anything that should have solicited such a reaction. She leaves at your request; you retreat to your bedroom and cry the rest of the night. In your frustration, you vow that no matter what, you will not go out again until you lose that weight!

Some days later, you have to go to the grocery store to get some needed supplies. You go way out of your way to shop at a store that is not in your area. This way no one you know would see you until you have lost this weight. Suddenly your worst nightmare is realized when a different friend catches a glimpse of you and starts to approach. Your eyes have made contact so she knows you have seen her, except, rather than continue approaching, you suddenly turn down another isle ignoring her. She feels wounded by your response and goes home and calls another person whom you both know. They get together and decide that you must think you are too good for them and you no longer want them as friends. This rumor spreads to all of your shared acquaintances and suddenly everyone is ignoring you—that is, everyone except your closest comrade.

There are so many stories circulating at this point that you don't know what the truth is and why everyone has suddenly turned on you. Your good friend tells you one story after the other of what she has been told. However, the one story that hurts you the most is the one where you supposedly told someone you were not going to hang out with her any longer because she was beneath you and you did not have time to invest in having friends that were such a low life. This story really sticks in your craw, and it makes no sense to you whatsoever; you would never say such a thing.

You have decided because of this that if they can make up stories, so will you. *After all*, you think to yourself, *you did not need them in your life anyway. After all, friends, real friends, don't do these kinds of things and spread false rumors.* So, in an attempt to support and validate all of your feelings, you begin creating your own stories. Your close confidant decides she too will ignore them. This is her way of showing her total commitment to you. She also wants to make you feel better. She then decides she will call all of her friends and tell them to ignore these people also.

The truth is, this is really no different from how a world war gets created—a much larger scale, but the principle is the same, my Beloveds. It is along these lines that the first discord was introduced to the Earth; even though the circumstances were a little different, it is still the same energy. I will address this more in another chapter.

You can see how much harm is done through one little thought gone wild. How could this have been resolved before it got so out of control? The person having the thoughts could have had some compassion for herself and then been okay with the 15 extra pounds, perhaps. Or, the person who arrived could have given her words a second thought before speaking. And last, what if the person who had gained the weight had taken accountability for her feelings? She could have said, *yes, I have gained weight; please help me find something that makes me look slimmer until I can lose it. Things have been very difficult lately. I really need your support to help me right now.* If any one of these three solutions had been used, everything would have played out differently.

People must decide what their desired outcome is that they want to create in their lives: fear and pain or peace and love. If one chooses inharmonious feelings and actions, everything and everyone who knows the person suffers. When peace and love are chosen, all will reap the reward. In the bigger picture, all actions affect the whole. Yes, you, my Beloveds, in your own world affect the bigger picture, for you are a part of All That Is.

The number of people present at my sermons of eons ago was low in comparison to the audience that one well-known speaker today attracts. Yet look at the effect the Teachings of the Father had upon humanity. Do not discount what **you** bring to the Earth.

Once the energy of discord is created, it cannot be destroyed; it can only be changed. Energy must stay as it was created until its creator learns how to direct the energy differently.

The above example helps to explain how an outward display of inharmonious feelings could bring about a war among friends. Now I would like to use an example to show you how the inward dialogue of inharmonious feelings can bring about an equally destructive force.

We will start with the feelings of *fear*. Here is the scenario we will be working with: *Today I have a job interview.* This is a neutral statement until we add a feeling to it. You could choose *excitement* or you could choose *fear.* Before discord was present upon the Earth, anticipation of something about ready to occur was experienced as something wonderful. After discord was introduced, it became a fearful expression of something about ready to happen. *Dread* was the emotion assigned. You have a choice of how you wish to experience *anticipation*.

If you, however, put fear with the anticipation of getting a job, you will have a dialogue that will create in-harmonious feeling. An example of this is as follows: *Oh no, I have a job interview tomorrow. What if they don't like me and I don't like them? I don't have anything decent to wear and I don't have the extra money to buy something. I wish I were smarter and looked a little more sophisticated. What if someone with more education beats me out of the job? I knew I should have gone for more education. I just hate having to answer all of those awkward questions. If I only knew what they wanted to hear, I would just say that. I wish I did not have to go, but I need this job.*

Self-talk such as this creates a lower vibration. Everything that comes to this person must match this energy. Therefore, the journey he/she has just created can only bring forth more issues related to self-worth. Unconsciously he has just formed the perfect self-sabotage. **All slower vibrating frequencies of inharmonious feelings limit the person in what he or she really wants to create**. The person really wanted this job, but because anticipation of something coming created fear, the person actually ended up with a vibration built on apprehension.

Continuing along these same lines, let's explore the next step the person is likely to take in the downward movement into negativity. The spring-board effect is now in full swing. Let's say the person did not get the job because when he went in for the interview, all of the thoughts he had been thinking were floating around in his energy fields. Think of these thoughts as balls filled with negative energy. Even though the employer could not consciously read the energy, he was able to intuit, to feel something inside himself that said, *No, he is not right for this position.*

Of course, it does not stop here. This person, more than likely due to his thoughts, will continue in the downward spiral to an even lower level. He will move deeper into self-doubt, creating one thing after the other, all the while wondering, what is wrong? If he could understand that discordant thoughts are the culprit, he could immediately change his life around. Through taking stock of the mental treadmill he was on, it would help alter everything coming to him in his future.

If anything like this is occurring in your life, make a choice the next time you start on your treadmill and say, *Shhh mind, be still and know that you are God and you are the creator of your destiny.* So many people blame God if their life does not run like they want it to. I assure you it is not Father/Mother who does this to you, for He/She is only capable of loving you and wants the best to be given unto you always.

Let us look at a different outcome that could take place if the person had taken control of his thoughts. Where fear had once stood, now excitement and anticipation of something new and different can replace the fear. This type of reaction will create a very different kind of an effect. In the excitement over just being offered an interview, he has begun to play with the feelings of what it would be like to work for this company. He is not concerned about what the employer will ask him. Instead, he has made up his own questions, pretending that he was the one doing the interview.

He/she practiced his replies daily to the various questions he had thought up until he felt confident in his delivery. It did not matter to him if these were the right questions or not. He just wanted to become more comfortable with giving quick and concise responses. Now that he had addressed the interview, on to the next thing—what to wear? This type of person will borrow what is needed if he doesn't have it. The more he thought about the upcoming interview, the more excited he got. This type of attitude becomes the catalyst for pulling to him what he desires. Let's say the interview went well but he still did not get the job. The employer calls him and tells him that they hired someone with a little more education. This type of person would say to the employer, *Thank you for letting me know. I would like to ask you if you know of anyone who may be looking for someone who would be interested in hiring a person who is honest and dependable like I am?* This person with this type of thought processes will get hired, if not at this place, then shortly somewhere else. However, the employer doing the interview may reconsider his decision.

I would like to approach this concept in a slightly different way. If you were to pretend that the Light that shines inside you was like a lamp without a shade, and the thoughts that you create were like a lamp shade, what do you think would happen if you continued to place layer upon layer of shades on top of the light? With the first few layers of shades, you would still be able to tell that there was a light there. Soon, however, as more and more shades were added, you would no longer be able to see the light. The light did not go out; it's still burning. However, the shades covered up the light to the point that it could no longer be seen. These shades are like your thoughts.

A chain of thoughts (positive or negative) will always be followed with a creation that matches that vibration; that is the Law. Anger and rage precede rape; love would never precede an action such as rape. All negative thoughts have to be dealt with at some point. All creators of those thoughts are held accountable for what they have created. If you, as the creator, do not deal with those thoughts and issues and choose instead to leave them unaddressed, they must go somewhere until you are ready to stand accountable for these actions. This is how emotional baggage gets created. The thoughts are stored in the emotional fields of the body. (This was addressed in the previous chapter.) **The person may not even be aware that he has stored emotional energy until it becomes ignited.** This can be a potentially dangerous situation. Domestic violence is an example of this. You have heard of cases where all of a sudden, someone, without warning, pulled a gun and shot a family member. They did not have a release valve in which to release their pent-up energy.

These seemingly idle thoughts have gone into storage as potential energy for the future. There they will sit until something comes along that matches that vibration, and then it will flare up in the form of an explosion. Or, perhaps the person has been successful, but only for a little while longer, ignoring his potentially explosive emotions. He continues to act as if everything is just fine. He does everything he can to run faster and further so that he does not have to face his uncomfortable feelings. Sooner or later, that keg of dynamite will be lit. Depending on who or what the circumstances are, it can vary anywhere from a yelling match to a world war.

That is unless you have made the choice to become accountable for your emotions and what they have created in your life. **Accountability for your own creations is the answer for avoiding explosions.** However, it is important to remember that it takes time to empty out the luggage compartment filled with emotional baggage. If you think it can be done overnight—that is highly unlikely—but not impossible in some cases. The energies of today are moving very rapidly and this is an advantage for you. What recently would take 20 years to accomplish can be done rather quickly now **if** you desire to complete these types of lessons.

The first few levels of emotional clearing can release rather easily. Often, people may find themselves feeling happy and free without those heavy belief structures hanging on. This new sense of lightness can lead a person to think that everything was cleared. This euphoria can even go on for quite some time. Then suddenly something happens in his life and the person reverts to a pattern that did not get totally cleared out. At first he may even feel lost and confused, feeling like all the work was for nothing. He may even say to himself, *But I already cleared that pattern. Why is it back?* Understand, my brothers and sisters, there are layers that must be peeled away—similar to an onion.

Let's take an issue like *love hurts* to help clarify what I am saying. In order to have a belief like *love hurts,* there had to be many different types of experiences that led to creating this belief. Each time that belief was reinforced, it created another layer in the person's emotional baggage. When a person finally wakes up to his/her beliefs and thoughts about a situation, this is when things start to change. Layers and layers peel away because of the person's willingness to address it. The more aggressive the person is in choosing to create a different outcome for him/herself, the quicker the baggage compartment is emptied. You are no longer attracting the mirrors of your beliefs back to yourself.

Negative emotions have created discord in other areas besides your own energy fields and or organs of the body. Discord is stored in the Earth's atmosphere: in the water, in the soil, and in your home. **The walls of your home hold the energy imprint of those living**

there. This is why fighting in the house can be so damaging, not only to those hearing the words, but also to the spirit of the house. **Walls hold the intentions and feelings of those present. That energy is held there until someone or something releases it**. Have you ever walked into a room where you suddenly felt uncomfortable? You are actually picking up on some discordant energy that is held in the walls.

Discord can also go into your food. If you are angry when you are cooking, it is transferred into the food. If you are eating out and the chef who was preparing the food is upset or perhaps is working at a job he does not want, all that feeling transfers to the food. When you partake of this food, you are consuming those emotions. **Through blessing your food, you help change the energy and release any discord that does not belong there**. This is one reason praying over your food was introduced upon the Earth. Another reason for praying is to remember the life that was given in order for you to sustain your body. In **Matthew 15:36**, you see where I, too, prayed and gave thanks for that which was given unto me: *And he took the seven loaves and the fishes, and gave thanks, and brake them, and gave to his disciples, and the disciples to the multitude.*

All of life is affected by the energy of discord. Nothing upon the Earth escapes. Even the Earth's atmosphere has an energy belt of sorts around it—it is called by many names, some of which are the *do-not-pass ring*, the *ring-pass-not,* or the *energy-seal*. The purpose for this sealing of energy around the planet is to protect the Universe so that humanity's discord won't be released into the realms of the Heavens. If this safeguard were not in place, you could have destroyed the Universe by now. As you begin to master yourself, you will be able to journey outside of this field of energy. This is how the new Earth will be created and the death and rebirth cycle of life ended. However, you must master your thoughts and emotions or you will not be allowed outside of this energy-seal until you do. It is all up to you. After all, you are the creator of your reality! (2013)

Remember what the scripture says in **John 14:2**: *In my Father's house there are many mansions; if it were not so I would have told you so.* The energy of Father is very expansive, and Earth is not the only domain where life exists. This is why it was necessary for a seal to be placed around the Earth.

The discordant energies stored within the great Mother Earth, created from wars and violence of the past, are currently being released. Think about all the wars that have been fought throughout time and the buried bodies of those souls who lost their lives due to this violence. What happens to the pain created by mass consciousness? Where do these emotions go? A good portion of this energy stays trapped upon the Earth plane until there is a way for it to be released. This energy is different from the stored energy I spoke of earlier that goes with you from lifetime to lifetime. That stored energy holds your personal lessons. Look at the Earth today and the discord that is taking place. Those energies are here to stay until a shift can occur within humanity.

Have you ever wondered what creates a hurricane? Science has a technical answer that allows the mind to make sense of what formulates this mass of swirling water and air; however, there is a spiritual reason as well. This disturbance of water is caused by the **emotions** released from humanity. *Fear* and *anger* created on a mass consciousness level will release this type of energy into the atmosphere. It is stored there in the Earth's energy fields until it is released back upon the Earth due to over accumulation. If you are wondering, my Beloveds, what kinds of emotions would create this kind of release, here are just a few things: war, fires, Wall Street, greed, hunger, economy, political difficulties, elections, terrorism. Literally, anything that humanity is emotionally upset about will create this type of release. The Law states that all discordant energies must return to their creators until all is cleansed and purified and brought back into balance once again. (*Hurricane "Sandy" 10-2012 devastated the East coast to the tune of billions of dollars for restoration.*)

There are various belts of discord that are stored **inside the Earth** as well. (Similarly, you have toxin pockets in **your** body.) These are stored particles of discord—emotionally charged energy—that are alive and are yelling to be set free from their imprisonment within the Earth. They cannot be released until a matching vibration comes along to cause a release, which often produces cataclysmic events.

However, there is something that can release these toxins from the Mother without harm to others. This neutralizing agent is LOVE! Through this action, the energy stored within her will dissipate when she feels the vibrations of love returning to her. There will no longer need to be cataclysmic events if humanity will but return to its natural state of love. When people resolve within themselves the real meaning of what it means to love, all will be brought back into balance. You cannot love another or even life, my Beloveds, until first you love the self. When you do this, you serve all of mankind and you help free the Earth from the stored vibrations of pain and suffering.

The more humankind takes accountability for its own life and feelings, the more **one** will affect the whole. Through the activation of your heart, you will unleash such a potent force that not even the most powerful atomic weapon would be a match for you. This ripple effect begins with those closest to you and then spreads out across the world. Everyone you touch with love and kindness touches another. Science has now proven how one isolated event can affect someone else in another room without there seemingly being any type of correlation between the two. This is called Oneness, my Beloveds.

It is also time for heads of governments to stand accountable as well for their creations; instead of blaming the other, work together for a solution. No good can ever come through the act of blame. Start fresh and let the past go. Be present now and work as One. (*The United States of America has just gone through an intense period of political elections 11-06-12 with President Obama being re-elected. The opposing party, the Republican, is having a difficult time in swallowing this sound defeat and few members are reaching across the aisle in Congress in cooperation with the President,* 2013.)

Think of your current-day yogis. Their energies are loving and peaceful. It is difficult to think any type of negative thought or feeling of anger when you are in their presence. This is similar to what will happen with the Earth as you return to love.

Ego has done much to contribute to the discord upon the Earth. However, there is another way to approach ego. Understand that **the reason ego wants attention and acknowledgement from others is because you have been too busy doing and not giving this acknowledgment to yourself**. When you are jealous of others or what they have, it is because you have not valued you and what **you** have. If you see your ego as a gift that helps you on your journey, it can become a great tool for self-awareness. If it were not for your ego acting out, you would not know when you have journeyed too far away from the love of self—where you connect with the God within. **Ego has no need to act out when you are taking care of the kingdom within.**

When discord is present, it brings forth a slow vibration. This slowness causes you to experience the shadow side of yourself. **Love is a fast vibration and brings forth Light.** As the Earth increases its movement into the faster vibrations, it will kick up the stored energy—the shadows of discord, the emotional baggage that you have stored.

Think of a glass of water that has sediment in the bottom of the glass. You cannot really see the sediment because it is stored at the bottom. As soon as you stir the water, the sediment begins to cloud the water. This is how it is happening upon the Earth. The stirring of the energy will begin to bring forth shadow and Light at the same time. This is already happening and will continue until all this sediment is cleansed. This change/clearing will help humanity alter its concepts about life, and out of that, there will be a very different way of dealing with situations; love will become the way and not war. Humankind will soon begin to understand the interconnectedness of life, and it is through this understanding that humanity will choose peace rather than the previous energy of discord.

I have watched humanity kill one another in the name of God. I have witnessed religious orders slander other orders—in whose authority do you do this? My Father brought forth many ways in which one might return to His Kingdom. Different religions speak to the needs of various people. I ask you to be the best you can be in whatever religious order you follow. As you honor Father/Mother, you honor your own creator-hood. **There is no true religion**, for if that were so, then God would only favor one and not the other. **God does not serve religion; religion serves God**. No matter where you attend your worship services, these are the Teachings to live your life by: love and honor God; love and honor yourself; love and honor your brothers and sisters; honor life and all of its creation; remember the Kingdom of God is found within. If these are the Teachings you live by, then the Kingdom of Heaven will be opened unto you no matter what religion you do or do not belong to.

I have watched words being spoken between husband and wife that tear at their hearts. I ask you, where in the scriptures have I taught you to harm the one that you love? It is best you say nothing until you are able to express your truth in a way that honors this union.

I remind you that destructive forces claim victory over mankind through the use of fear and control of another. Do not be blinded and fall prey to these temptations.

If you come up against those who would harm you, call me forth to stand in front of you to shield you with my Golden Light. Invite me in daily to help illuminate your mind and your heart that you may know the truth of all things. Decree it and I will come.

Man has not yet learned that true power is a co-creative process. *Power over* is no longer the way. Discord enters in through the solar plexus when one wants to control another. If you are in a situation where someone is attempting to control you, ask that I help stand as a protector over this chakra. Seek those out who desire cooperation and union rather than dominion.

My Beloveds, all that I did upon the Earth, even in my own passing, was to teach you. My death showed you that your spirit lives on. There were those who did not believe that life was eternal. I came to the Earth during the darkest of all times to show you the way of love. This provided you with a template so you would know how to exit the darkness of discordant energies.

I tell you that no human should have power over you. There is only one way and that is to seek the truth within so that you may return to your rightful place in the Heavens. Become the living, loving Light that you were meant to be. Do this and the doors of Heaven will open up and blessings unnumbered will be poured out upon your heads. Through these blessings, you will be given the opportunity to have everlasting life. **The physical body died due to accumulated discord, but this need not be any longer.** Focus upon life and love and not upon death, and through this, you will bring to the physical body the attributes of everlasting life.

The slower vibrations of discord are what create deterioration of the body and lead you to the door of death. However, if you choose life, love and peace, death no longer needs to be and you will continue to live on, transforming yourselves into your Light body and obtaining everlasting life. You will continue in the same Higher State as I, while being alive in your enlightened form, if you so choose. I ask you to live life in love and peace as I showed you and you will no longer have karma. I ask you to live beyond the human creations of limitation. I ask you not to focus on what you don't have, but focus on what you do have and more will be added unto you. I ask you to LOVE.

My brothers and sisters, speak your truth; honor yourself, but do so in a way that brings respect to all. The day is soon to arrive when you will no longer desire your way to be forced upon another. Respect for all will be at hand and the Universe will become your playground once again. We will be as One.

Your brother Jesus (Jeshua ben Joseph)

How to Release Fear

*You cannot release fear until you first feel the uncomfortable feelings that are associated with it. Allow it to come up and consume you, if need be. Stay with it and welcome it. Say, "Ah fear, you are welcome here. I know you are afraid of (fill in the blank). I love you and want you to allow **you, fear,** to have your voice." As you stay with the fear and allow it to reach its climax of expression, the next step after that is it will suddenly disappear. It no longer has any* *energy for you allowed it out. Then decide where you want to put the energy that you were using to feed fear, to keep it alive.*

Do you want *to create the same thing again or is it time to create something new with this energy? I am not saying feeling your fear will feel comfortable; however, you will set yourself free because the fear no longer has anything resisting it. Play the scene out in your mind. Allow yourself to say and do in your mind whatever it is you are fearful of. Once it is expressed/played out in your mind it will begin to dissipate. Thinking the thoughts will not make you do the act. However, telling yourself you are wrong and evil for having such thoughts **will create** the negative energy in your body and energy fields, thus creating discord to build again. The only thing you have to fear my Beloveds is fear itself. Remember fear is false evidence appearing real. You cannot help what enters your field of experience, for you are a part of all things. However, how long you keep it (thoughts and feeling) there is where the issue begins or ends.*

Jeshua 2013.

5-A

LUCIFER'S GIFT

My Beloveds, before you begin this chapter, you may want to go back and revisit what I said about the chair (*Introduction pg. xviii*). I have asked you to read this book using the chair as a metaphor—an example of how one's perspective can change depending on the view from which it is seen.

Mankind has misunderstood the great gift Lucifer has brought forth for humanity. If you look at the name Lucifer in Latin, from which the English word is derived, it means *Light-bearer*. We are going to explore my brother's gift to humanity in this chapter.

I will start by using the metaphor of the diamond mine and how diamonds are mined. Diamonds are formed deep beneath the Earth's surface. They are pure carbon that has been placed under immense pressure for millions of years.

A technique called *liberation* is used to free the diamonds from the ore that surrounds them. This process uses radiation to detect where the diamonds are located within the ore. Sensors go off and flashes of the diamonds are exposed through the application of radiation. The diamonds are then easily detected and extracted from the ore.

Diamonds are not only clear but come in varying colors as well. For this teaching I will use the pink diamond* because pink is associated with the loving energy of the heart.

The diamond mining process works to uncover the jewel found within the stone, not any different from the process which mankind goes through to unearth the love within. When you have freed your heart from pain and judgment (emotional baggage), you will have discovered the rarest of all gifts, your own Divine and loving heart (the pink diamond). Everyone must go through his/her own personal mining process in order to receive *liberation.* The *liberation* I speak of is the freeing of oneself from various beliefs—one such belief is that you are evil/bad and not worthy of love. The truth is you are a loving God-Creator, and you were born from a loving God Father/Mother Creator. Therefore, you cannot be anything but Love. It is through your own liberation process that you will uncover YOU!

The pink diamond and its mining process are being used to help you understand the mining you must do to connect with your own heart. The color pink represents Divine Love, and Divine Love is who you are at your core. All the colors of this Earth had to first come through the vibration of Love (which is represented by the color pink). All shades of experiences that you go through must also pass through the love of the heart in order to heal. When you heal, you gain mastery and are then able to return to your I AM and Father/Mother God Creator.

Lucifer's gift to humanity has been through helping humankind experience its darkness inside itself. He is the bringer of Light, for you cannot understand the Light unless you understand the dark—they are both sides of the same coin. There is a tribe called the *Kogi* located in the Sierra Nevada de Santa Marta Mountains in Columbia. They understand that in order to free the heart you must go into the darkness. Their leaders are selected when they are first born and are called *Mamos* or *Mamas*. They spend the first 9 years of their life in dark caves learning all they need to know from the wisdom within. They enter the spiritual world of *Aluna* and there they learn how to create what is needed. Unity Consciousness is

56

their way of life. They help guard the heart of the world—the Great Mother Earth.

This is the gift Lucifer brings to all who are willing to understand. Just like the pressure applied to create the diamond, **darkness within helps the human Being find and refine him/herself.** Humanity has been given free will, which allows you to choose those lessons that would serve in your own journey into mastery. Lucifer agreed to provide the energy/pressure needed for this lesson.

The shadow can tempt you, but it is by your own free will that you make the choice to partake. Lucifer has been greatly feared, as well as faulted and judged, for playing the role of the dark; yet someone had to be willing to play the role or there would never have been the experience of duality to know oneself. Only through the refinement process can the pink diamond of your heart reveal itself—just like there would be no diamonds unless the pressure were applied to the carbon that creates this precious stone.

Let us explore the part of the diamond mining process called *radiation*. The procedure used in the mines is much the same as the method used to temper the human spirit so your gifts can be seen. The Great Central Sun (the center of the Godhead) is located in the heart of the Universe.** At different times, the Earth receives rays of intense Light from the Great Central Sun in order to assist with the evolution of the Earth and its inhabitants. When these rays are received, everything upon the Earth is affected. That includes the physical body as well. There is a stirring that takes place within each person. This Light triggers the tri-fold flame of the heart. The flame is what connects you to your I AM and from there to Father/Mother.

This Light when received can be experienced as pressure in the chest or it may trigger deep-seated emotions to arise. Jags of crying spells are often associated with the release of this kind of energy. And sometimes it is just an over-all feeling of discomfort. This same Light can also trigger earthquakes or other Earth disturbances. Through the experience of your brothers' and sisters' traumas, no matter what kind, it triggers this Light within the heart to open. You feel compassion for those in need and you begin to band together—Unity. Through such an event like this, you are left changed and spiritually more open to the Heavens. This is similar to the mining process when radiation is used to detect the diamonds.

The release of rays from the Great Central Sun is done with great care and assistance—just like the radiation that is directed towards the ore must be done with great care. The Great Central Sun has Cosmic Angels that assist with the releasing of these rays. Humanity often refers to these Beings as *Ascended Masters*. It matters not what you call them; it only matters that you understand that there is great assistance being given to help you uncover the rare gift you have within. All work in tandem with the Great Central Sun.

When I walked upon the Earth, I worked with the rays from the Great Central Sun in helping those around me see the truth of the words I spoke. Rays were released through my own body to help humanity heal, as well as to help me perform the miracles. These rays connected me with **their** own I AM.

Perhaps you can now understand the *liberation* process that is used in helping humanity and the Great Mother Earth free herself from her own limitation. The act of letting go of limitation gives you *liberation.*

Without Lucifer going into the darkness with you, the pressure needed to help you *master yourself**** could not have taken place. I, as well as others, came as Way—showers to help you find and master yourself. I ask you to ponder these questions: Are not all mining operations staffed with workers who work underground in the dark? Are there not workers who work upon the surface as well? Can a mining operation be successful without both existing? **My work as Jesus Christ was to oversee the mining operation from the surface while Lucifer agreed to take some of the workers and go underground (inside the soul) to make sure that the mining was successful.**

The time is drawing nigh when the mining operation will be closed down. Those who have been deep within playing the role of darkness want to return to the Light. You can help them feel comfortable by releasing your fear and judgment of those who stayed underground. Remember, you could not be who you are without their help.

As Jesus, I never taught *judgment*. Yet humanity has judged my brother Lucifer. All of my Teachings were of *love*. They still are to this day. How can the miners (the darkness) feel safe to see the Light within them unless those who stayed on the surface stand in love and acceptance of that shadow, which is you? Can you see that by accepting the shadow within, then the dark can accept its Light without? All the darkness really wants is to be understood and not judged. Only you can do this; no one can do it for you. It is your own fear that prevents you from loving both parts of yourself. The only reason darkness attacks you is because you are holding the energy of fear and judgment. When you stand in love, the darkness releases and realizes its mission is accomplished and then it can start to see its own Light.

When I journeyed into the wilderness as Jesus, my brother Lucifer tempted me just as you are tempted. The key word here is *tempted*. He never forced me to do anything, my Beloveds. The same is true for you. You are never forced to do anything you don't really want to do. The shadow only presented to me another option to consider, but I always had the choice. I appreciated what he did as the holder of the dark because it helped me refine and commit deeper to my own mission as a Master and Way-shower. I want you to understand that the temptations I spoke of are not literal, but instead they were my own battle within—that is where the conflict resided.

People often think that I, the Master, was perfect. What I will say to you is that while I did not have personal karma (thus your ideas of perfection), I was still part of the mass beliefs/perceptions that create karma; this is why I experienced temptation from within. Remember, I was born into human form, and no matter what belief structure you hold to today, you know I **had** a form and that form had the DNA of the past within it. When we speak of karma, I want you to know that personal karma is only a small percentage. Mass consciousness is the majority of the karma and affects all of humanity. **My temptations from the dark side came to me to help me master the mass consciousness that I was a part of. As I mastered this part, it helped humanity as a whole.** This is the internal work that I did that is not talked about.

You cannot find your center unless you have opposing opposites through which you can locate your midpoint. If you think you are evil, then there you will stay. If you think all you are is love and Light, then there is where you will stay. Neither position allows true freedom, for both beliefs keep you in a prison of limitation. To think you have never done anything evil is an illusion. To think you are all evil is also an illusion. You will continue to reincarnate until you finally understand that **you are both, Light and dark**. When you make peace with both parts of yourself, then you are free.

I remind you, Lucifer took the inward and I took the outward. The tool that Lucifer uses to create the inward pressure is *judgment* and *fear*. Through mastering this part of yourself, you become like the rare pink diamond, and then through the *liberation* process you are set free. The tool that liberates you is *love*, and by following the teachings of love and non-judgment, you are set free. What would this world be like if suddenly all of humanity quit judging? Think of the many ways you have judged those who you know and love, including yourself. I ask you as you become aware, don't judge the judgment; just notice it and make a choice in each moment to shift that judgment into a space of *acceptance*. When you do this, you will find the midline, your neutral point. It takes practice, but you can do it and each time you are successful, you will find you have created a new pattern, which ultimately will lead to total freedom and out of duality.

Before I close, I wish to address one more thing that you may be thinking about. How do you find forgiveness for the drunk driver who killed your child, or the child who was subject to ritual abuse or raped? ***

Yes, my brothers and sisters, I understand the pain such loaded experiences create. Your journey here upon the Earth is to learn how to balance and master the emotional body. You can only do that through the act of non-judgment and love.

Let us use the example of a child being raped. Your rage and pain are out of control and you cannot console yourself. You want that person to be caught and punished. Let's say the person **is** caught and punished, but you are still in rage. Perhaps the reason your rage is continuing is because you want that person to feel your pain like you are feeling it. I will tell you that even though the person is not you and perhaps at this moment in time he/she may not be feeling what you are feeling, there still will come a time when there will be an adjustment made. **All discord must be neutralized, no matter**

what the act against another is. This neutralization process occurs through an act of bringing all deeds forth to be viewed by the person who has done the act. You refer to it as a *life-review* upon death.

Consider this if you will: sometimes an act such as this takes place because the victim in this life was the perpetrator to that person(s) in another life. It is not up to you to be the judge. Your mission is to surrender it with the knowing that the Father/Mother God Creator will bring about the best way for this to be dealt with.

Let us look now at why you might have chosen to be a party to this kind of act. Maybe it was because you wanted to work on how to make choices around judgment and rage. Remember, mirrors reflect life back to you that which you are in need of healing. When you were designing your life's lessons for this lifetime, you were approached by the loved one that you would see raped. This loved one said to you, *I am going to be raped during my next life; I have a debt to pay back. I see that you want to work on rage and judgment. Would you like to team up so we can help each other learn our lessons?* This is when you made the decision to have this experience, my Beloveds.

When an experience such as this happens, this is when the darkness, Lucifer, will present to you the opportunity to continue your rage or not. You will have equal opportunity of choosing the teachings of love and letting go and letting God resolve the final outcome. Having the choice is what creates the pressure. (Remember how the diamond is created deep within the Earth.) You may find you desire both roads. The pressure of having two choices causes you to battle deeply inside while addressing both the shadow and the Light in tandem. It's your free will as to which path you will take and how long you will stay on that path.

Neither Lucifer nor I judge you. We only show you two different options. If you choose Lucifer's way, then you will stay on this path a little longer to learn your lesson. You are not yet quite ready to discover that rare pink diamond located in your heart. If you decide to choose love, this will allow you entrance onto the road of Self-mastery. This road sets you free, and soon you will have mined the beautiful Light (*gemstone*) within your own heart. At this point the Heavens will say, *Welcome home; we have missed you immensely!*

Remember you **are** love; you are **loved** and you will return to love because nothing else exists.

I AM Jesus/Jeshua ben Joseph, your brother and friend.

* PINK DIAMOND: Extremely rare and once were only available to royalty. Out of the millions of carats mined at Argyle (Australia) yearly, only some 700 have been found to have the quality of a pink or red coloring

** THE GREAT CENTRAL SUN: This is considered to be the center of the God-Head. It is the Sun behind the Sun and is the heart of the Cosmos. The Great Central Sun is One with every individual's own I AM Presence—his or her God-Self.

*** MASTER YOURSELF and *Forgiveness of Self* are discussed and presented in the Appendix.

5-B

THE DARK SEED

It was not always the Earth's journey to integrate such extremes of Light and dark. It was a part of humanity's journey, however, to understand itself and how energy works. The depth and the extent of the darkness (Father's shadow) had never been experienced upon the Earth to this degree before the Dark Seed arrived.

Planet Earth was seeded through what is called *Starter Seeds*. **There have been a total of seven Starter Seed Races upon the Earth**, each one from a **different planet**. The first three and some of the fourth Starter Races did ascend. The mission of each Starter Race was to learn how to integrate its own Light and darkness, although it was not as dense as it has now become. Through the various mastering of each individual, in that particular Starter Race, he or she would reach his own alignment, not only individually, but as a collective, thus assuring his Ascension back to his God state. His entire journey upon the Earth was only to last for approximately 14,000-15,000 years, give or take, and then the next Starter Race would start to be born upon the Earth.

It was during the fourth Starter Race that the Heavenly Hierarchy, along with the I AM Presence of those already upon the Earth, decided to bring forth billions of life-forms that had become lost in their own shadow. They had become so dark that no other planets were willing to take them on and help them out of the dark. They had even destroyed their own planet and had been suspended in the in-between worlds until something could be done or someone would be willing to help assist them. Hence, they are known for this writing as the *Dark Seed*.

For these souls to make their transition, it required just the right circumstances along with the Light workers who felt they had the tools and strength to carry this plan out. Not just any planet would work to bring them aboard, for it required a planet that was working on polarity integration. This is when those upon Planet Earth decided to step forth and offer their assistance. Once they came into the Earth plane, it became more difficult for those who were here already. Not even the Heavens realized that the darkness could take hold to the degree it did. The Heavens watched as humanity worked to integrate this darkness into themselves and thus bring the Light to this darkness.

The energy of fear began to take hold of humanity. Fear only exists in the third and fourth densities, or dimensions. Originally, the first three Starter Races vibrated in what is called the fifth dimension and higher. The fifth dimension (5D) is free of this type of fear. It just does not exist. The energy of something about ready to arrive in the Higher Realms is experienced as *anticipation.* However, as the energies dropped in vibrational frequencies, because of this integration of the dark seed, the fourth Starter Race and those thereafter dropped into vibrations which forced them to spiral into the third dimension (3D).

An example of this would be if you had a lamp-shade with a 100-watt bulb under it. As you use the 100-watt bulb, the light shines out. This is equivalent to being in the fifth dimension. However, as you place one layer of blanket over the lampshade, instead of having the light from the 100-watt bulb, you have the light of a 60-watt bulb. If you keep placing blankets over the bulb, you have a 30-watt on down to what looks like zero wattage. However, underneath the blankets there still is pure Light.

The subsequence Starter Races were not prepared for the amount of darkness they were encountering. Soon they lost sight of their own mission and their own Light within. Consequently, humanity became lost in the same darkness as the Dark Seed had been.

Fear began to take hold of the minds and hearts of humanity. I shared in a previous chapter, *The Energy of Discord,* the different ways one could approach an interview for a job, positively or negatively. *"I am in anticipation of something wonderful happening when I go for my job interview, for I know they will be excited with what it is I have to offer"* Humanity lost its own knowingness of its Divinity and the ability to feel anticipation. **Anticipation is born out of the knowledge that you are loved by Father and that all will work out for your best interest.**

Now you have an understanding of what happened upon the Earth, as you embarked on the journey to help integrate the Dark Seed and bring them back into the Light.

Consequently, the fourth Starter Seeds, or Root Race, did not make its Ascension on time. Instead, even to this day, many still are present upon the Earth. However, the fifth Root Race still came in; then the sixth Root Race and now you are embarking upon the seventh Root Race. The seventh Root Race consists of those with higher vibrations that will help you in ushering out the darkness and bringing the Earth back into balance.

I want humanity to understand the gift that was given to all. Those who have taken this journey helped the Dark Seed integrate and bring into balance their own Light and dark. What a great opportunity for them to have been given this. You have been successful no matter what some may choose in the end; many will have returned to the

Light. The doorways will all open soon between 2012 and 2030. **No one will be left behind now unless they so choose.** Today the Earth looks much like it is in chaos, but I remind everyone that out of chaos comes order. As each one of you awakens, you will ascend out of the density of darkness. You will help move your friends and your relatives along the way also.

In the fifth dimension, you will no longer have to earn a living through the sweat of your brow, for a new Law takes over. That Law requires all your needs to be provided for. Why is that so? It is so because you now have learned how to let go of the energy of density/discord and instead you are bringing forth the energy of the Presence which is Love—through Self-love—thus allowing it to flow freely through you. That is the gift. When you allow the I AM to flow freely through you, you release the chains that have bound you for lifetimes, allowing the Universe and the Heavens to open with blessings unnumbered poured out upon your heads.

Remember what I said so very long ago: *I myself can do nothing but it is the Father (the flow of Divine Energy) that does the work.* You will see once again the Earth return to a place of balance, free of the storms and the weather conditions that are now present. This will happen as your own internal storm of Light and dark comes into balance. In other words, the blankets that were placed upon the lamp will be removed from your Light, and you will once again shine and your lives will be joyful and filled with love. (2013)

(Chako: It was at this point that Jeshua stopped channeling and asked that I write a story about an experience I had in my youth that would add even more clarification for Beloveds as to how a simple judgment statement from another could still arouse pain many years hence. This true story is played

out through humanity and shows how deep the dark energy
is embedded into a person from the careless thoughts and
remarks of others.)

I grew up during the depression years. In 1933, my parents bought an old Victorian house built around 1879. The house had two stories and had 14 rooms with 14-foot ornately carved ceilings. This house became my parents' passion. My mother spent hours at auction houses and brought back treasures with which to enhance the Victorian beauty. One of her finds was a beautiful Baccarat crystal chandelier which she hung in the room she named the *Library.* Behind the Battenberg lace draperies in that room, I was allowed to create little villages made out of colored clay that I placed on the 4 windowsills in the bay window.

I grew up in that house from the age of 6 to 20 when I married and then moved away with my military husband.

To me, this beautiful mansion was just a home where I played dolls, slid down the banisters, jumped off the back stairs, seeing how many stairs I could leap off of at one time (5), and where I never bothered wearing shoes. I was oblivious to other people's comments about our beautiful home, for many times I would be out on the front lawn pulling up dandelions that not only helped the lawn but became the green vegetable for that night's dinner. We kids (my sister and two cousins) earned 10 cents per hour and filled our buckets gladly for that was our movie money for Saturday's matinee.

Our home grew lavishly with my mother's beautiful acquisitions and the sweat of her brow. She spent many hours steaming and scraping off old wallpaper, but few people realized this labor of love. They only saw the finished product. We kids matured and entered high school where it was a cultural shock to mingle with other students who were not as fortunate as we were.

I started hearing murmurs and remarks about me. *"She thinks she is so good; she is stuck up."* What people did not realize was that I was extremely shy and intuitive. I could feel their judgments, and yet I never knew why they disliked me or were jealous of me. I liked them! I just wanted to be friends. It was not until I was older and had traveled to many distant lands that I knew it was not me, but that I was a mirror to people of what they wanted and did not have. If one thought, *"she thinks she is so good,"* that was a mirror of that person thinking she herself was **not** so good—her jealous ego churning its venom.

(As Jeshua and I looked at this dynamic, and he repeated what the person had thought and had said about me, I immediately felt tearful and experienced the pain that still resided there. That energy of the dark barb had lain and festered with its hurt and pain for over 50 years! It had surfaced when the same remark and energy had been repeated once again in the present. He suggested I call in the Forgiveness Prayer and not only forgive the other person but forgive myself for all the years I may have suffered from that careless judgment of my youth.

As we did the step-down process with the veils closing off memories of Light-filled times, we became more enmeshed in the darkness. We no longer had the ability to recognize what was our darkness or someone else's. Therefore, our victim-egos matched the energy and played out the same game on others. It is only when we realize that we are Light and have called in the Forgiveness Prayer that these dark nooks and crannies of yesteryear can be transmuted into the Light within us. And another blanket has been removed from our lampshade.) Chako: 10-29-10.

6

MOVING FROM DUALITY TO ONENESS

This is a pivotal time here upon the Earth; many changes are taking place—changes within you and changes within the consciousness of mankind. Humanity is on the brink of a massive awakening. My Beloveds, some of you are the forerunners of this awakening. Individuals will awaken at a very rapid pace during the years of 2012-13. Many of you who obtain the knowledge of what this is all about will be in great demand as Wayshowers for those souls that have not yet awakened. You have struggled these last five to ten years but there will come a time, very quickly now, as you join together in 2013 and 2014 that your struggles are over. Many of you will be vibrating in the Higher Realms and therefore, you will no longer suffer as you have. Instead you will find that your dreams will become realized. You will experience the Nirvana of life. (2013)

You are bringing yourselves into balance within the Oneness. You cannot do this until you find your neutral place within—the neutral place is located in the heart. To accomplish this you will be required to bring chakras one through three into balance with the fifth through the seventh chakras. They will meet within the heart (4th chakra) to create the love and peace that you so desire. This is what creates the balance and out of that place the Unity chakra (located outside of the body) is created. And Oneness is realized. I want to remind you that all that you are, all that you can be, is the Divinity of your own I AM. This is what will bring you the joy that you desire. Let go of the little will and rejoin the greater Will of the Father.

I use the term *Father* to describe this great and loving Energy that flows through everything. Father is all encompassing and compassionate. Father never loves one of his children more than another. Father never judges, for all He is capable of doing is to love. There is also a Father beyond the Father that I speak of (Great Source Creator). However, it is enough for us right now to deal with the Energy through which you desire to connect.

The Father you wish to connect with is personal and hears your prayers. As you join with your own sacred heart, you bring a balance into your life—much like sitting in the center of a compass. You can see the value north, south, east, and west brings. This is what you do when you are in your heart; you witness the experiences of the first three chakras as well as the upper three chakras.

Living in the heart allows you to witness your negative and positive thoughts without making one better or worse than the other. This is what Father does; He sits and is a witness to all experiences without making any of them wrong. You stay out of the drama and out of duality of good and evil. You sit in the middle of your own heart and witness the experiences of your own life(s). The more you do this the more you will become the observer of your own Divinity. (2013)

Duality began in the step-down processes, my Beloveds, in order to experience oneself outside of the true Law-of-Love. Now you want to experience **Self** back **in** the true Law-of-Love, **out** of Duality. Therefore, there will no longer be right or wrong as you make this journey back into love. Each of you will find this neutral place of being—a place of loving all experiences—much as we Ascended Masters do when we witness your dramas upon the

Earth. One day you are in happiness, and the next day something else occurs and you are in sadness. We witness you and your drama without participating in your journey. The day will come when you will witness your emotions without their being labeled as *good* or *bad*. It will just be the way it is for that day.

It is important for you to grasp the concept that all experiences are there because you created them so you would have those experiences. The more accountability you take, the freer you become.

There are so many levels to love, peace, joy, and happiness. You have spent many lifetimes in pain and sorrow, and now it is time to join the Light that you are. You will not do this from a dualistic point of view of first experiencing Light and then dark and then Light and then dark and so on. You will have full acceptance that all emotions are okay. This is what allows you to journey deeper into the place of peace. **Your own I AM Presence is the flow of the energy of Light within you**. This Light of the I AM comes in through the sacred heart which helps bring into balance your own Light and dark. It thus illuminates the mind, bringing an understanding to all of your thoughts. This is what will lead you into *forgiveness,* for you will finally come to understand there is nothing to forgive. You were only allowing yourself to experience the many faces of you or I could say my Beloveds, the many faces of God! (2013)

Through the process of duality, you became separated from your sacred heart. You could think but you could not really feel your true self, for you judged that kind of feeling. You felt that allowing your heart to feel deeply only opened the doorway to pain; so you kept yourself shut down/walled off. This is why right now there is so much pain upon the Earth. As the doorway opens fully to your own hearts, all that has been kept bottled up must come out. Hence, it may come rushing out! (2013)

This is why there is so much drama right now upon the Earth. Humanity is **feeling** finally what it has not felt but judged for eons of time as *weakness*. Some of what you are feeling is fear; fear of feeling your hearts. As the heart-rose opens and reaches its full bloom, you will begin to attract the things you desire into your life instead of the things you fear. (2013)

Each time you choose **peace** rather than discord and fear, you make a statement to your authentic-self that you wish to sit in the center of the compass of your own life. If you only look in the north direction, you see no value in the other positions. However, when you sit in the **center of the compass, your neutral zone within**, you note that all the other positions are experiences and just as valuable. This is when you start witnessing another person's life and instead of judging what he or she is doing, you will find yourself saying something like this: *Who am I to say that what he is doing is not right, for he is the creator of his own experience(s)?* You cannot determine for another his or her journey. You can say only *what is your source—truth?* After all it is all about you and **your** journey not anyone else's.

In order to return to the Higher levels of being and to have the peace that you desire, it requires that you stay neutral—in your heart. Neutrality does not mean you do not care; it means you still have your passions, but you are so involved in bringing forth **your** joy, **your** harmony, **your** love, **your** Light, that you no longer are focused on anyone else and what he or she is doing. This focus is not from a place of ego—for it is not possible for ego to be here in a negative way—but from a place of centeredness within. In this position, you no longer find the need to make another wrong so you can be right. That was duality! This is how you marry duality. This is what this next stage of development will be—the mastering, the marriage of the male and female parts of yourself—bringing yourself out of duality and into the Oneness.

Therefore, what is going to happen on the Earth is that many of you who want to be in relationships will now be able to have relationships, but not in the old paradigm way. In the old paradigm, you had a relationship in order to mirror to you what you could not see inside yourself. That is why there was so much drama and discord involved.

In the new paradigm, because you have brought the male and female energies into balance within yourself, your desires to have a relationship will now be based on *balance*. Humanity is still not done with the opposite sex, or the same sex relationship journey—this type of experience will still continue for quite some time. However, there are some who will not desire to partner. Therefore, he or she still will make the marriage commitment of the male and female within but will join with the I AM Presence in a singular fashion. (2013)

It is a beautiful journey that you are embarking upon. When peace is obtained within the heart, this is what activates the DNA to vibrate at a frequency that will bring you all of your heart's desires. All of the cells within the body recognize the Divine energy pattern from Father and thus they react accordingly.

My Beloveds, are you ready to cancel the contract of duality? If so, repeat the following command statement out loud:

In the name of the Lord Jesus Christ and through the power of my I AM Presence, I command that the contract of duality—the tree of knowledge of good and evil—be broken, canceled, and thus voided. I am no longer willing to take part in the human game of

> *duality, nor of this tree. Let it so be written in The Book*
> *of Records. Thank you, Amen.*

Now repeat this out loud:

> *In the name of the Lord Jesus Christ and through*
> *the power of my I Am Presence, I now choose of my*
> *own free will to only partake of the Tree of Knowledge*
> *of Love and Oneness. So be it and let it be written in the*
> *Book of Records. Thank you, Amen*

It was a soul agreement to experience duality. Contracts are not written in stone; they can be re-negotiated as the soul advances in its understandings. You are now free in each and every moment to make the choice not to judge. If you judge and stay there in the judgment, you will take yourself back into duality. If you find yourself slipping and you judge something, do not worry. Just say *cancel—cancel* and you will release that judgment before it can create anything in your life. Try as much as you can to stand in the center of your compass and witness life from a place of observing. Remember not to be hard on yourself. For within the imperfection there is perfection. (2013)

Now let me address the building of the New World, for it is being built on love, peace, and harmony. It is built as each individual soul brings forth within its own person the joy that is his or hers for the claiming—whatever it is you wish to accomplish will come to pass. You are not going to be held at bay anymore from your passions and desires. The gateway is opening now so that you can live out that which you want. The only requirement is that you ask yourself in each and every moment, *am I doing what I want to do? Do I believe in my joy and myself in this moment?* If you do not, then ask yourself where you are not in alignment with the passions of your heart. Ask what is required of you in order to live in the passions of your heart. (2013)

You might be in a job that still is not quite what you want. Ask yourself if you are all right staying in this job for a little while longer. If you get *NO*, then I ask you to explore what is stopping you from *jumping off the cliff* to do what you really want to do! If it is fear, then you are still dabbling in the old reality. Fear is what will shackle you once again. You also can command it to exit your life. Remember you are the creator.

In the name of the Lord Jesus Christ and that of my I
AM Presence, I will no longer buy into the illusion of fear.
You no longer have power over me. I take back my power
from you and I command you to leave me NOW! Amen!

That is what you would say to counteract the fear—*You no longer have power over me. I will no longer take part in that.* Can you feel the shift within you as you say that? You have that right; the old Law is done for many of you—the old Law of being held captive is over.

In the Higher Realms, you must have boundaries, my Beloveds, for how can you join Oneness until you are clear about who you are and what your truth is? Joining in love, peace, harmony, and hope—all these various states of Higher Frequencies of being—cannot happen until you are strong inside of you and know your selves. Again I will say, until you have boundaries, you cannot let go and truly join Oneness. I will give you an example. (2013)

Let us say we are creating a wonderful tapestry. This tapestry has a picture woven into it—a beautiful colorful scene. There are trees, animals, and people walking in a picturesque town built in and amongst the trees. Off to the right you see another scene of several people sitting on their porch swings watching others as they walk by. You are also able to tell through the placement of light that it appears to be about noon. The tapestry brings you a sense of peace. **This** is a tapestry with boundaries. If you have no boundaries in the tapestry, all the colors would bleed together. So you see, you must have boundaries or it does not work to join Oneness, and it would not be the kind of reality you would enjoy living in.

This is what happened in the past—the step-down process into the 3D world. You listened to what everybody else told you that you should be doing and thinking. When you have boundaries, you are clear with what your joy is and to where your heart is. As you are clear within yourself, those of you who resonate with that same frequency will be pulled together. It is not a right or wrong. There are many different levels in the Heavens—many different frequencies. This allows everyone to experience life in the way that brings in happiness.

That is why when you become neutral, the neutrality allows everyone to have his/her experience. If everyone can have his/her experience, there is no need to have a rebellion against rules and regulations; there are no longer those who break the law, because they can have whatever experience they want.

If you have a group of people who want to murder, and you have a group of people who do not want to murder, those with no desire to live in a murderous community will pull to them only those who want the same experience because they are choosing harmony without making the other choices wrong. The non-judgment is what keeps you in these Higher Frequencies. It is not anyone's right to judge another, my Beloveds, for that belongs to Father. I speak now of the Higher dimensions, not that of the 3D. In the 3D, you had to have a different kind of law in place to keep some sort of order.

When you have defined boundaries and are very clear as to what you wish to achieve and where to go in life, you will create that. **What you focus your attention on is what you will achieve.** If you focus on negativity, if you focus on fear, you will have that. The New World is not based on these lower vibrating frequencies. You are learning now how to turn these negative traits upside down and focus instead on what it is you desire. This is what attracts the Realms of Light and allows them to open to you.

As you settle into the fourth and fifth dimensions, you will find that those who want the same things you want will gravitate to you. Those who want more density will stay in the area that allows them to feel most comfortable. That is the creation of the New World. That is what's next—learning to master yourself. Now that you are popping up into these new realities, learn how to maintain that. (See *Master Yourself* in the Appendix.)

Yes, you might pop down momentarily, but you will pop back up. As you experience life getting easier, you are not going to want to pop back down into discord. You are going to learn that it is through the affirmative, focusing on and giving attention to the things you do want and not what you do not want that brings positive results. The things you do desire in life come to you. Everyone wants an easier life. Everyone wants to be in more joy. Everyone wants to giggle, laugh, and play. Everyone wants to be free of struggle. You do not focus on struggle in order to get free from struggle. You focus on the freedom; you feel it in the body. **It is what you give your attention to that creates it.** It will become easier as the density falls away.

We in the Heavens have always been and will always be here for you. It is my personal promise—that there is not one of you who walk during these last days who I do not walk with. I will help if you will do a small portion—just a small portion of the work. We, the Ascended Masters, my Apostles of old, all of us, will step in and do what we can to lift the greater burden from you, if you will just do a portion of it. Through the desires of your heart you will be successful, my Beloveds.

There will be many things in the world that your TV and other forms of media will want to scare you with in the final stages, as the old falls away. They have done their part. Laugh at their fear but not in a way of making fun of them. Laugh as though they are children acting out. They are so frightened that they will not have anyone to play with any longer in their creations of drama. As you watch children when they are throwing a temper tantrum, you see the little two-year-old is stomping his feet and crying because a toy was taken away. You know how you find humor in that and yet also compassion. You took the toy away not to be unkind, but perhaps it was because it would have hurt the child in some way. You did not take away the toy in maliciousness, but in a loving, caring, and gentle way. But the child interpreted it as a brutal thing. This is the same reaction from the Beings that you are moving away from now—the detached entities who prefer to continue to stay in the dark energies.

In taking away the toy—**you** are the toy—you are removing yourselves to these Upper Realms that will bring you more joy, peace, and harmony. Therefore, the dark will act out like a child, for they are fearful that if you take away their toy, they will not know how to find a way to play appropriately. Now you are saying that you no longer want to be their toy. Instead you are saying, *I want to grow up now and accept accountability for myself. I AM truly a God-Creator. I AM truly me, my I AM Presence.*

With that understanding, you open the flow to the Upper Realms, to your Creator-Self. As that energy flows through you, it lifts you into the arena of the heart. It is now the time of opening the heart, my Beloveds. However, as I said earlier, for some who have had their heart locked for eons of time, there is a great deal of pain that must come out. Others of you have already unlocked your heart. The unlocking of your heart leads you to love deeper than you ever have loved, but not without boundaries.

The old paradigm was to give, give, and give. But this is not the experience for the new paradigm. The new paradigm is to love **you** first—to love and to accept all that you are and to celebrate you. When you fill your own cup first from within the love found in the heart, then you have much more to give out.

If this were interpreted in the old way, it would sound selfish. However, you are rising above these types of views. No, what I speak of is the place within where you connect with Father and not with man's views of these words. The New World is where you give to yourself. If you need to eat, you eat. If you need a car to drive, you have one to drive. You no longer have the desire to own multitudes of everything because you are filling yourself up with the Light now from Father. That is the New World. (2013)

There still will be things that go on in the world. There will be energies of discord at times that you will feel. Please do not judge those energies; stay as neutral as you can. Be in peace. The fourth dimension can be a difficult dimension as you move through that. There is a great deal of disembodied souls in the fourth dimension (4D). Therefore, as you pass through this phase, they are going to want to glom onto you. It is still a place that holds fear as the mass consciousness shifts.

As quickly as you can, focus on moving to the fifth dimension (5D) level and give thanks that you are leaving (4D) quickly and easily. However, do not judge this level, for it is an experience only. You never can avoid a dimension, but you can move through it with ease and grace. Be like the bird, the *roadrunner,* as he is running down the street. Move as quickly as you can from some of the things that might get stuck on you. You just hold your focus. The more you stay in the neutral zone within yourself without judging another, loving compassionately, even if the person is unkind to you, all the while keeping your boundaries in place, you are allowed to move beyond 4D and into the fifth dimension. Once you do this, then the need to interact with the old realities will vanish. This is when you also will have the communities I spoke of earlier.

A further explanation of 4D is that you will find people returning to their strong Christian or religious ways. Understand that that is a fear place, because they do not know what is true or not true. Therefore, they will turn to the teachings of their religious orders in order to feel safe. I am the One who ushered in Christianity. There is nothing wrong with this, so do not judge it. They are doing this because this is where there is a sense of peace and belonging. They will one day understand the entire truth of all the various and different steps that lead back to Father.

I brought forth the Light and one day this will be fully understood. When the true teachings that I brought forth are fully realized, humanity will once again embody its true Godhood state. It will no longer buy into the control others have placed upon my teaching. My true teachings are to honor yourself—honor the flow of the Father working through you. As you honor these aspects, you will honor your brothers and sisters as well. All the miracles, everything I performed, were not me, Jeshua, the Christ upon the Earth plane. I, as a human Being, could do nothing. The Father, His flow of Energy through me, does all things. I performed such miracles to demonstrate this flow of Energy that was Father so you would know how to do the same.

Humanity in its need to control others had a way of twisting some of my words. It took out much of what I had said and in other places inserted more of what would serve its needs. I do not stand in what you would call *judgment* of this, for even though this was done, it still served the greater picture. So, in fear humanity will return to its roots. However, Father's Light will not allow people to become lost again. They will awaken to the truth, for Father and I will move within the hearts of all. All truths will become known through the inner planes and not the outer planes.

The Second Coming is within each and every one of you. That is how **I will walk with you again, through your inward knowingness of me.** I will not come again as a Christ child to be seen and worshipped. *Been there, done that*, as the saying goes.

Religion of old will eventually come to realize the true teachings of love and the beliefs of hell, fire, and damnation will disappear, for all will come to understand the real mission of Lucifer and me.

I would like to clear something up for humanity. When I was tempted while wandering in the desert, who do you think was tempting me? Can anyone tempt me except me? What I was speaking of in the Scriptures was my own temptation of self—that duality that I had taken on when I came in.

Lucifer is a Being that exists on a different dimensional realm. This is a Higher Aspect of him from the Earth Being called *Satan*—just like my name is *Sananda* in the Higher dimensional Realms. Lucifer, my brother whom I love dearly, had another part of himself that became **Satan**, who you have also called the ***devil***. Those **are the step-down names.**

However, when you put Light and dark together, what color do you get? Gray. So, for this example we will say that Gray is equal to Oneness. Oneness encompasses all emotions, all feelings. Going back to the example of the center of the compass and using that concept and me as Jeshua and Satan as the devil, you can see that when we come back to the center of the compass what you will have is a place that is called *neutral*. In the Higher Realms, Lucifer and I serve on the same team. If you go higher than that, we are One.

The place I speak of is no longer bad or good because it just is and that Is-ness is God. There are many levels inside of the Energy of Oneness, my Beloveds. So the teaching here is to learn how to marry, to love, to embrace your Light and dark so you can emerge out of duality. You may be saying, *but Jeshua, it feels so awful to feel those emotions.* It feels awful my Beloveds, because you judge these thoughts and feelings. If you would just embrace them and say, *Ah my friend, my shadow, you are feeling very angry right now and you want to hurt something. I can feel this raging anger inside of you* (which is you). *Let me hear everything you want to say. I will stay and listen to you.* Become the observer; do not join in the anger—just observe it and allow this part of you to have its own voice. Again do not try to fix it; just allow it. As you allow it, you will find this helps to dismantle the rage. Then just love yourself for having had those feelings. Look into the mirror and say to yourself, *I love you; I accept all of you; thank you for trusting me and allowing me to feel these feelings.* You are talking to the parts of you that have not been able to express themselves. You will be amazed at the changes that will start occurring within you because you no longer discount this part of yourself.

No longer play the *devil's advocate* with yourself, my Beloveds. No longer allow the mind to rule you. When you put the mind and the heart together, you have the heart that illuminates the Presence and the mind that carries it out in the physical realms. **Mind tracks**: get up, get bathed, get dressed, get breakfast, and keep appointment. **The heart illuminates that which you desire to do and gives the mind the power to carry it out.**

The former way would be that mind shuts down the heart and the ego kicks in. *Look what that person has; why can't I have that? I am going to take it from him/her; after all, I deserve it more than she does.* However, the new way is to activate the Divine Mind—your Higher Aspect Mind, your God Mind, the Greater Mind of All That Is—because that is what you find when you open your heart.

Returning to the example of the compass, let's say you are now in the center of the compass, and you have been successful in marrying the Light and dark within. You have married your own duality. *What happens now you ask?* Ahh, you experience the many facets of being and exploring the bliss—that energy of pure love and acceptance begins. This is what awaits you. We do not even know in the Heavens what this new change is going to bring because this has not been done before. This is why it is called the *GRAND EXPERIMENT.*

You will finally understand forgiveness—forgiveness of yourselves and forgiveness of humanity. You can now unlock the perpetual state of reincarnation, for enough of you have awakened. You have experienced enough in regards to playing the same game from different vantage points over and over. The game of chess is done! It is love and forgiveness that frees your souls and will continue to unlock those places within your hearts. It is through the heart that the new is built upon the Earth. A new Earth based on very different principles.

There will come a time when those who no longer want to dabble in duality will be fully separated out. You are already feeling this;

you will gravitate to groups that will support where it is you want to go. As you sojourn to these various levels within you, you will begin to build and live your dreams. These dreams were given to you so you could bring forth the new upon planet Earth. Focus on what it is you want; do not give attention to what it is you do not want. Even if what you do not want is presently in your life, do not focus upon it. Only focus on what it is you do want and you will find that it will become easier and easier to manifest your desires.

How does God work? Remember you came from God and when you return to God, you will do so by moving deeper into Father's vibration of Peace and Love. You will find a profound realm of silence here—the kind of silence that is deafening to the human ears. And yet it is filled with such a profound peace and knowingness that it lulls you to sleep, a deep slumber that allows you to rest in the Energies of Father.

You leave a small part of you outside this deep place that I speak of, waiting while you sleep in these loving Energies of Father until you renew yourself. *Why do you leave a piece of yourself outside this state of bliss*, you ask? So you can find your way out when the time comes to awaken and journey once again into a new experience. Who knows what it will be the next time around after having succeeded in the human experience.

What is it like to join in the forever silence of Father, the Great Creator? You are a thought and your thoughts are joined with all the others who are there resting in the Great Silence. In human terms, you would say you are no where and yet you are everywhere and in this profound state of never ending peace and bliss. (2013)

I want you to understand that God has a God, who has a God, who is a part of the (deep place I just spoke about) Great Creator-God, which is Source fullness. You have always been a Creator using

86

Father's Energy to create with. What has never been done before and was done with this creation, the human form, is to find its Godhood and bring it aboard while still being human and having a form in which to experience its God-Self moving around in and through itself. This has not ever been possible to bring aboard the full expression of God to experience touch, smell, along with all the other pleasures you get to experience as a human **and** to know its shadow-self as well. This is not to say the Father-Source no longer exists in Its form, or that the other Gods no longer exist. No, all is still in existence; it is just that now there is a new addition to the family that can live on and on if it likes. The Heavens are changing because of you, my Beloveds. Many of you maintain a memory of what it is like to be back in Oneness. That is why so many of you are striving and wanting Oneness energy and yet you want to maintain individuality, a situation that has caused somewhat of an inner war for you.

Humanity thinks that Heaven is the final answer to everything. My Beloveds, **you** are the answer. **You** have created this. **You** have changed Heaven. **You** are the mountain because you took the Oneness energy, brought it into a form and now are changing every experience every God has ever had and will have from this point on. Heaven will never be the same. Out of this, other Universes are starting to pay attention, because now God really can experience Itself as never before.

Many of you have been told that through your journey here God gets to experience Itself more. Perhaps now you can understand why. You have taken free will, you have taken the neutral Energy of God, you brought It into a form, you learned about the shadow side of God, you helped free souls who were trapped for eons of time, you have brought to the surface the Light and the dark in a beautiful marriage through which you birthed a new Being, a new human God-Being. Can you see why the Heavens honor you so?

You are creating a New World; what you are creating no one knows exactly because you are changing all of the rules by which this game will be played. So where this phenomenon will go, who knows? Through living within your heart, your creations will continue to maintain the integrity of Father, which allows this creation to succeed and move into realms never explored. You hold within you, as you awaken, the God-Code and it is all found in the human DNA. Yes indeed, Ye are all Gods!

I, Jeshua, come from this energy, and it is the Energy of Father that I used to help jump-start your DNA 2,000+ years ago so you could remember and awaken to who you are today. This is why Father gave these words to you to help trigger something within you to pay attention to: *Behold, this is my beloved son in whom I am well pleased.* If Father had not done this, you would not have paid attention to my words and teachings in the same way that you did. Now I, Jesus/Yeshua/Jeshua, chose to do the step-down process like you did—to become human so I could do the work that I needed to do. I stepped in; stepped back out, playing a part. I want you to know that I had many lifetimes before being Yeshua as well. **I was also Adam, and Eve was Mary Magdalene.**

I am coming through different teachers bringing the same truth but in various ways, to help awaken you. This stretches you to see me, not in the ways of old but in a new and different manner, which furthers your awakening process—for knowledge is the Kingdom of Heaven. The knowledge I speak of cannot be accessed until you have your heart opened, and then it will illuminate the knowledge given with the understanding of the Father. You are beautiful Beings and you have done it! Now let us keep with the practicalities of what to do each and every moment so you can continue to grow.

You are not just one God, my Beloveds; you hold all the secrets of the Universe within you—all of them in all Universes outside of this one! Within your own God-Self, you are a part of all the Gods that have ever been. That is quite an amazing thought to behold. As you stay in your heart, you will feel Father's Love supporting you and that Love will reveal all things, as well as give you the strength to continue the process of returning to all that you are and all that is.

As you grow and develop beyond the stages of the dramas of life, you still will need to watch yourself and not allow the self to fall back into highly emotionally charged situations. This does not mean you do not care; it only means you do not carry others' emotional dramas for them, for only they can solve their own creations. Instead, you are to become the observer; however, do so with compassion.

See them finding the answers to their problems and give thanks to the Heavens that they are finding their way out of the drama they have created. Help only if you are prompted by the Holy Spirit; or if they ask and it feels right to you. This is the only way, my Beloveds, to really help another. However, each time you choose peace for yourself, each time you choose neutrality instead of the drama, you have taken yourself further from having to experience any of these types of situations. Thereby, you help the whole to heal itself. If you worry who will be there for them, know that Father and their I AM always will send someone along to be of assistance who is the perfect vibration they will need to help them.

The Beings that are still in the shadows are afraid to have you awaken. Once you have awakened, they will never get you back and they know that. Yet it is your awakening that helps them see what they have been afraid of seeing—they are Light also. That means they have to decide whether to stay in the shadows of the darkness or to awaken.

It is similar to your family systems. You might be the first one in your family system to awaken. Everyone becomes angry with you because you are making things uncomfortable for them. You won't play the role you have always played. Your refusal to play the same game changes things and they become upset. So they try to convince you that you are wrong.

However, you now can see with new eyes and therefore, you refuse to be manipulated. Here is a sample of the language that might be spoken verbally or non-verbally: *How dare you look at your roots; how dare you look at the skeletons in the closet. Why did you say NO to me? How could you do that?* And guilt is always a good manipulation in family systems to throw into a confrontation in an attempt to control you.

But, my Beloveds, this is really no different than what the darkness is feeling and does to you also—except they do it slightly differently. Darkness will try to convince you through fear that you are bad or not worthy etc. The lesson is still the same. **All family systems have a Lightworker in them to help bring Light to the darkness in their family line.** In spiritual family terms, they are referred to as the *Great White Buffaloes,* although in the traditional family unit, they also could be referred to as the *black sheep* of the family. This does not mean that others in your family do not carry the Light in their DNA, for everyone has both in them. It is just there is always at least one black sheep in the family. Or, I could say, *they dance to the beat of a different drum.*

The world to come will be very beautiful and filled with love. You will have harmony, the joy that you want; all your dreams will be realized. At the 2012 gateway, you will move through a portal which facilitates the great change and thus the new begins. As I have said before, there will be shifting of dimensions. This is just the beginning.

Here is a story about the channel Cynthia and what changing dimension could look and feel like at times in your own life. She often has great difficulties in riding the different dimensional levels that are now being presented to her in her own life. However, in time she will learn, as you will learn, how to move with ease and grace.

She had a flat tire so she called AARP to send someone out, and they said the man would be out in 40 minutes. She waited, and when the man had not arrived after waiting 40 minutes, she again called AARP. The receptionist replied that her husband called and cancelled the request because he would fix the tire. Cynthia told the lady on the other end of the phone that she had no husband and asked what number he had given. AARP told her the number and it was Cynthia's phone number. Cynthia reiterated that she had no husband and she still needed someone to come and fix her flat tire.

Well, she got her tire fixed, and we told her she had shifted dimensions and had forgotten to bring all of her issues back with her to get resolved and to go back to where that dimension was when everything first happened.

You can move through several dimensions. For clarification purposes, let me state that within each dimension there are sub-levels of that dimension. This is what was happening to her. She was moving through these sub-levels. You can always go back and forth in the sub-levels of the current dimension you are in. However, you cannot go higher than the dimension of where your mastery lies.

Let me say it this way for clarity. You may be in 5D realities in the future, but some of your family members are vibrating in 4D reality. They will not see you unless you, through intention, drop your vibration in order to be seen. They cannot go to 5D if they have not mastered themselves sufficiently to live in 5D realities.

For some of you by the end of 2012, when you reached the next level and take up your new roles as the Avatars for the New World order, you will cease to be seen by some people. It is not that you are not there; it is just that the other person is on a different plane of existence and his/her brain is not able to register your presence. In other words, you will become invisible. And **you** will not see these other realms unless you desire to be seen or your work requires you to be there. So you will be living in a different plane of existence, all the while having gone no place but only into a different frequency. It is just like the angels; no one can see them here. Some of you can see me (*Jeshua*), but not all of you can. You might see me in this body, for that is why I use another's body in order to bring you these messages. But there will come a time when you will not need me to teach from someone's body, for you truly will be living and walking in the same realms as me and all of the angels.

This does not mean you will go beyond where you will need food. However, the body may require food of a different kind, or not as much. More than likely sugar will not be something you will consume in these realms, nor will you consume coffee. However, you will decide what you want.

If gardening brings one great joy, by all means, garden, for there will still be plants. If that is not your expertise, you can just say, *give me a banana,* and the banana will materialize, for you will know how to do that. You did this back in Atlantis and Lemuria. You focused upon what you wanted, and suddenly it would appear. Or you may not want to eat at all; you then will consume the Light. (2013)

There are many different experiences. If you wish to travel, you will no longer need a car. You can think of where you want to go, and your molecules will disassemble in an instant and reassemble at your destination. (*Bi-location*)

Beloveds, keep in mind that for those who believe in hardships, as many do, they will experience that, for their created reality will be instantaneous. All will go through the 2012 gateway. However, according to your thoughts, you will have very different experiences from each other.

A question was asked during the class lecture about the energy changing in the Sedona, Arizona, region. I explained that in the Four Corners area (*where 4 states' corners come together: Utah, Colorado, Arizona, and New Mexico*), the Light comes in to be distributed around the world. In Arizona, because of its desert qualities, it is all about death and rebirth. The summers blaze and you are constantly re-birthing yourselves in a way that does not take place in rich forests, for the energies are held differently there. Arizona is where transformation can take place.

I will speak of Prescott, Arizona. There are many Lightworkers who will be leaving that area because it is time for others who are coming up (*Jacob's ladder*) to hold the Light there. There will be those in Sedona leaving also. Sedona will maintain its Light, but there is a movement to the Phoenix area because the darkness wants to take out that area since Arizona holds so much Light for the rest of the world. We had Cynthia move to the Phoenix area because I can work out of her body from there. There are small pockets of dark in Prescott and Sedona, but the Phoenix area holds a greater population, and the work needs to done there now so that the Light is not tampered with. The dark has tried to tamper with the Light in Arizona.

I am speaking of duality, not in a way to take you back into that, but to help you to understand. Stay in the center of the compass and listen to the teachings. The dark is afraid. If you are bringing Light to the rest of the world, there would be no question as to why they would want to take out your area. The more of humanity that awakens, the more the dark cannot control and is then lovingly brought into the Light.

It has been a joy and a pleasure to be with you. You are magnificent Beings. Stay in your hearts and enjoy your journey here.

I AM Jeshua ben Joseph

7

ILLUMINATED OBEDIENCE

Illuminated obedience is brought about when one understands the Laws of the Universe. Humankind has learned through blind obedience to obey the lesser laws so that they might obtain *illuminated obedience*—the Higher Laws of God. As I speak about illumination, it will be as an expression of the expanded self. As the world changes, you will come to know of this expanded self. There are two aspects to every person: there is the human and there is the Divine I AM. Illuminated obedience comes about when the human and the Divine join together—like a marriage.

However, there is also an illumination that occurs as you grow and develop on the Earth plane. For clarity between the two, I will refer to that type of illumination as *Earthly illumination.*

When you think of *obedience,* you think of it as being told to do something. If you are obedient, you do it; if not, you are called *rebellious.* You have traffic laws that tell you how to drive. You are obedient to those laws. There are laws that have been set up by your government; you are obedient because the lawmakers are the ones in office.

Obedience means cooperation with life, the laws and mankind. There are two levels of cooperation. The first level is mankind's ideas of what cooperation is or is not and the second is God's. Both contain blind and illuminated obedience. These levels of obedience are achieved through your growth and development. An example of this on the Earth would be if you were the one making the laws.

You achieved this position through a lot of hard work. Now you are able to create the laws that enforce safety for all. This is an example of Earthly illuminated obedience. Blind obedience occurs when people follow without full understanding of what all the laws are about; yet they know and trust it will serve the whole. These Earthly experiences teach and help prepare you to follow the spiritual laws so that one day you will be able to join your expanded Self—your I AM. Just like in the example of the traffic laws, blind obedience preceded Earthly illumination. However, there are times when blind obedience must be reexamined because it no longer serves.

Let's address *blind obedience* in relationship to family patterns. Some of you are still running these patterns that have been passed down from one generation to the next. You do it without even thinking. I will refer to this as *blind obedience*. An example of such a pattern would be as follows: let's say it has always been your job to have Thanksgiving dinner at your home, whether you wanted to or not. You never questioned it. Your mother did it and now this tradition has been passed on to you. It has always been understood that the first female born in the family would have the responsibility to have everyone over every Thanksgiving. So year after year, without thinking, everyone, including the extended families, would come to your home. You spend days getting everything ready. The idea of breaking the tradition never occurred to you. My Beloveds, there is nothing wrong with doing this year after year as long as you are making the choice to do it from a position of being truthful with yourself. If you are doing it from a place of fear of what the family members would think and say if you suddenly broke tradition, this will not help you spiritually advance from *blind obedience* to *illuminated obedience*

The above example applies to many things like old outdated laws that need to be changed to support the people of today. As humanity grows and changes, so must the Earthly laws. The Laws of the Heavens also change, my Beloveds, to support mankind's development spiritually. Remember the saying, *as above so below.*

After the year 2012, you entered into a new cycle of Laws, one that is based on freedom for all. Knowledge and greater spiritual awarenesses will become available to the masses. This will begin the process of the merging of the human and the Divine.

What precedes *illuminated obedience*? It starts when you give yourself permission to make choices based on what feels right for you in your **heart** without guilt. You begin learning that you have rights and that you are just as important as the next person—you have self-worth. You start accepting responsibility for all of your choices. You understand that everything in life comes about because you created it through your thoughts. This is when the change begins. You awaken and begin to align the human self with your I AM Presence, together in union. This is Heaven and Earth within becoming united.

The point I am making is that inside all of you, there is a Cosmic Moment that will come in your life. Whenever this moment arrives, you will be set free from all the chains that have bound you. Suddenly, you will make choices differently because your thought processes have changed. When it arrives, you may wonder what just happened to you; you may feel awkward inside and a little lost. Do not be afraid, my Beloveds, because you have just stepped upon the golden path of awakening and the union of these two parts; the journey has begun. It matters not what the catalyst was that created the Cosmic Moment. It only matters that you **allow** it to happen and unfold.

Here is a simple example that demonstrates *Earthly illuminated obedience*—but it works the same for your awakening into the Higher Spiritual Realms.

As a child, you cleaned your room because your parents told you to do so. You did not understand why that was important and often fought them in the process. However, you did it because you did not want to suffer the consequences. Now as an adult, you clean your bedroom because you can understand by hanging up your clothes and being organized how much better you feel. You also have come to realize that when your room is clean, you sleep better and awaken with your thoughts clearer. You now understand the wisdom of your parents' teaching. There were many stages of development from childhood to adulthood. Each developmental stage was vital to bring you to the understanding you have today concerning order and its importance. This we will call *Earthly illuminated obedience.*

I remind you it is no different in the spiritual realms. Eventually, you will come to understand the bigger picture. As the veils are opened, you may find you are conflicted between what has always been taught and the new information coming in. You are actually moving from one level to the next, my Beloveds, and this is something to celebrate rather than be afraid of. It will be a process and no two people will have the same experience. Each person will have his or her own Cosmic Moment at a different time and place than you. Therefore, do not expect others around you to necessarily understand, especially if you are the first one in your circle of friends to awaken. It will take a few years for this awakening process to complete itself. It is your time to know the truth because you have sought it. The mass consciousness has reached the point of no return—so eventually, everyone will be joining you.

The basic Laws of God are taught first through blind obedience. This is necessary to build a foundation in which you can understand the Higher Laws. Moses was a great example of what I am speaking about. Let us return to the time of Moses for just a moment.

When Moses went to speak to the Lord and left the Israelites camped at the base of Mount Sinai, he gave them instructions to follow while he was away. Moses was gone for 40 days and nights. During his absence, the Israelites became impatient and lost faith that he would return. In their state of fear, they returned to their old ways and started making a calf out of gold that could be worshipped. They held a festival and bowed down before this calf and began to honor it as their god. Upon Moses' return, he became angry at their lack of faith and broke the tablets containing the Ten Commandments. *How could they live these Higher Laws if they lost faith when he was only gone for 40 days?* So a new set of Laws was given to Moses for the people.

These are the Laws, my Beloveds, you still live by today. However, it is time to begin to live the Higher Laws. Enough of you have had to call forth from the Heavens and demonstrate your willingness to live your lives differently in order for the next level of awakening to occur. The call had to be made as a group collective, referred to as *mass consciousness.*

The first set of Commandments that Moses broke was the Higher Laws. These Laws would have taught the Israelites how to master the human ego-self and begin living in *unity consciousness—the* I AM Presence. Arch Angel Michael sought Moses out while he was in the desert and taught him about his I AM Presence. Later when Moses went up to Mount Sinai, the Laws were given that would teach the Israelites how to return to the Divine—the I AM. He was instructed to share this with his people. However, upon his return, it became clear that the Israelites were not yet ready. **Faith is what is required to live the Higher Laws**. So a lesser law was created—the Ten Commandments. Have you ever wondered why Ten Commandments and not Twelve? That is because the number ten is actually a one, which is symbolic of returning to the Oneness of all things. **The Ten Commandments were designed as steps that would teach the Israelites how to master their *ego-self*.** We spoke about *ego* in a previous chapter; however, there is something else I would like to add at this point. Ego is housed in a layer found between the human and the spirit-self. It will not allow you to pass to the Higher Realms until you learn the Law of Love—moving from ego-love to the spiritual-love. Actually my Beloveds, ego is your friend. I say that because it will help you to redefine yourself over and over again until you are ready to return to your true and natural state of self love. Love is the answer and has always been, my Beloveds.

Let us take a look at what the **Higher Aspects** to the **Ten Commandments** are:

1. "I am the Lord your God, who brought you out of the land of Egypt, out of the house of bondage. You shall have no other gods before me."

   Higher Aspect: Place no one before your Father/Mother Creator and your I AM Presence, for when you honor God, you honor yourself.

2. "You shall not make for yourself a craven image, or any likeness of anything that is in Heaven above, or that is in the Earth beneath, or that is in the water under the Earth; you shall not bow down to them nor serve them, for I, the Lord your God, am a jealous God, visiting the iniquity of the father on the children to the third and fourth generations of those who hate Me, but showing mercy to thousands to those who love Me and keep My Commandments."

Higher Aspect: Create not a false god to worship; look instead to the only true God, your I AM and Father/ Mother Creator. Do this and your soul will be freed.

3. "You shall not take the name of the Lord your God in vain, for the Lord will not hold him guiltless who take His name in vain."

Higher Aspect: To condemn God is to condemn yourself.

4. "Remember the Sabbath day, to keep it Holy. Six days you shall labor and do all your work, but the seventh day is the Sabbath of the Lord your God. In it you shall do no work—you, nor your son, nor your daughter, nor your male servant, nor your female servant, nor your cattle, nor your stranger who is within your gates. For in six days the Lord made the Heavens and the Earth, the sea, and all that is in them, and rested the seventh day. Therefore, the Lord blessed the Sabbath day and hallowed it."

Higher Aspect: Seek time to rest and find your balance; in this sacred inner place, you will hear the guidance of your own Soul—the Voice of God. Allow all others to do the same.

5. "Honor thy father and thy mother, that your days may be long upon the land which the Lord your God is giving you."

Higher Aspect: Pay respect and appreciation to all who have given you substance—Father/Mother Creator, I AM, Father-Sun/Mother-Earth, Earthly Parents.

6. "You shall not kill."

   Higher Aspect: Take not from your brother or sister their life's essence, for it belongs not to you.

7. "You shall not commit adultery."

   Higher Aspect: Lust not after something that is not yours. Instead seek the Light of your own Soul, your I AM Presence. If you do this, you will no longer lust after anyone or anything, for the spirit of God will fill you up. (Adultery is an aversion because you do not want to see the truth.)

8. "You shall not steal."

   Higher Aspect: Seek not what another has, for all your needs will be provided for if you will but trust and have faith.

9. "You shall not bear false witness against your neighbor."

   Higher Aspect: What you say about another is what you say about yourself.

10. "You shall not covet thy neighbor's house: you shall not covet your neighbor's wife, nor his manservant, nor his maidservant, nor his ox, nor his ass, nor anything that is thy neighbor's."

Higher Aspect: Seek within that which you seek outside.
Then all your desires will be fulfilled, for nothing can be
denied you.

My Beloveds, know that through your obedience to the Laws of God, you will know the truth of all things. Humbleness is the means by which you will gain your eternal freedom.

Your brother, Jesus—Jeshua ben Joseph.

8

THE BUILDING BLOCKS OF LOVE—THE CREATION

Love is the fundamental building block by which everything comes into form. The macrocosm is the template for the microcosm. To explain the creation of the Universe and the world, I will use the metaphor of how a building is built.

First an idea is born, along with a desire to bring that thought into form. In the building of a Universe, the *idea* is represented by the Father's Energy—the Divine Mind that is God. *The Mother—the feeling center of the heart, the creative side—represents desire.* This is the Father/Mother God Creator. It is through this union (idea and desire) that creation is allowed to have a form.

When you build a building on the Earth, you hire an architect. The idea must be translated to something others can read; this is called the blueprint (road map).

When the blueprint is drawn, you are ready for the next step. Now you hire the builders or construction company. The construction company hires the sub-contractors and so on.

Let's backtrack now and establish the reason for creating the planet. The idea and desire was to create a place for duality integration (two separate parts returning to their unified self) to occur. In order for this plan to work, there needed to be a world created where humanity could work out mastering its opposing sides (the Light and the shadow) within itself. When the individual soul finally balances these two sides, peace is the result. At this point you remember the truth of who you are—the *truth* being that you are born from love and are Gods, and because of this fact, love is all that is possible. Remember, **love is the building block** through which all was created and that is what you must return to. This inward knowledge connects you back with Father/Mother God Creator and to the Oneness of all things. Thus, polarity integration occurs and duality ends. This, however, is not just something I can tell you, for it must be experienced. It's the inward journey of putting the two halves back together that allows you this deep connection and knowingness. All souls must reach this stage in their development—the polarity integration.

When these two very powerful and highly evolved Cosmic Beings of love came together with idea and desire, the plan was born. A call was put forth through the unified power of the Father/ Mother God Creator for an Architect. This is what is called the *Cosmic Guardian. A volunteer* steps forth to hold this position. He/ She agrees to hold within His/Her consciousness the Light pattern for the planet and solar system that is being created. This is referred to as the Divine Blueprint. I might mention that everyone who responds to the Divine call does so out of his or her own free will and desire to be of service to the Creator.

Next, Father/Mother draws to Itself Its construction team. This team consists of a Planetary Guardian along with the *Seven Elohim* (Elohim means Gods): This is why there are Seven days in your week. **Hercules, Cassiopeia, Orion, Purity, Cyclopea, Peace, and Arcturus.*** These Beings act as construction workers and begin the process of creating the Earth just as the construction team builds a building. The Elohim begin to create through bringing together Light rays from the Great Central Sun (Father's Energy). At the point where the Light rays intersect, creation happens—like rubbing two sticks together creates fire. If we use the Earth's example of creating a building, this would be like taking two boards and putting them together using nails which create the walls of the building. **In the Heavens, it is Light rays intersecting that create the form and intention that holds it in place.**

The next step in the building process is to explore who the sub-contractors are in the Heavenly Realms. Just like on Earth, it is not possible for the contractors to do all the work. They hire out to *sub-contractors*. Sub-contractors take care of electrical, plumbing, dry-walling, etc., on the Earth plane.

This is why there is a need for a *Planetary Guardian.* The Planetary Guardian holds the blueprint for the Earth, just as the Cosmic Guardian holds the blueprint for the Universe. The Planetary Guardian holds the energy in a more focused way. Planetary Guardians are just like the sub-contractors for a building. Therefore, they must focus on their particular part of the electrical system of an edifice, rather than concentrate on the building per se. Once someone responds to the call to be the Planetary Guardian, it is time to complete the project.

The last call is for *helpers*. This is for those who will oversee the work directly. These helpers are the Archangels, Chohans, Guardians, Seraphim, Cherubim, Divas, and Elementals. (There are many Beings within each of these categories that are not being talked about; they serve in silence.)

There are many levels to creating this planet that I have not fully gone into. I have kept it simple so that you can grasp the concept and relate it to how things are constructed here upon the Earth. The important thing to remember is this creation was brought into being through love. Everyone who helps does so out of his or her own desire to be of service, and it is done in great joy.

Now for a minute, let us review what it would look like on the Earth if we were completing a structure. As we look around, we realize that there are some finishing touches that need to be completed. You realize that the walls and flooring still need to be decorated before you can open for business.

The finishing touches for building an Earth are to give life to the planet. This is done through the energy of the Sun, which helps foster life. Yet there was another need. It was decided that a self-training course that allowed everyone to work at his/her own pace and maintain his or her free will would be ideal. Through using the 12 signs of the Zodiac (which present both the positive and negative traits of that sign), each person would have ample time through various lives to learn about the Self and master these traits.

Now the Earth is ready to become inhabited. So Father/Mother God Creator put out a call for life forms to come and inhabit the planet. Your existence did not begin when you came into the physical form. You have always been. Your birth into this Universe came through the Light rays of the Father/Mother intersecting. Consequently, the Light of the Father/Mother exists within every individual. This is called the *Tri-fold Flame of the Heart*. As you return to the love of your own heart, you return to the Tri-fold Flame, the Mother/Father, which activates the individual God-flame.

The whole purpose for this experience is to accomplish polarity integration—remember the training manual for your journey here upon the Earth.

It is time to let go of everything that does not match the building blocks of love and return to your authentic Self. You **are love** and you **will return to love** and you are **loved.**

Your brother and friend, Jeshua.

*   The 7 Elohim are referred to as male in gender. However, they are perfectly balanced in the he/she energy and represent both. They do have counterparts just like you do within yourself and without (often times referred to as *twin flames*). These counterparts separate out from their original state as they drop closer into the Earth realms to help hold the energy for the game of duality.

**   Listed below are the 7 Elohim and the energy that they hold. I, Cynthia, have added how I have used their energy in my own daily life to help me grow and develop.

Hercules represents God's Will and is the guardian who oversees the energy as it is released to the Earth for use.

> *I have always had a strong connection to Hercules. Whenever I needed to accomplish something that was beyond my ability to do so in the mind or body, I would call upon him. He always shows up and asks me what it is I need. (He already knows.) When I tell him, he comes into my body where I have been blocked or unable to do something. Suddenly, I am freed up and am able to accomplish my task without effort.*

Cassiopeia is referred to as the God of Wisdom. He directs and governs the actions of *illumination* (clarity of thought) and *comprehension* (concentration of thought) which allow one to achieve full understanding.

> *I call upon Cassiopeia when I partake of the tree of Knowledge and Oneness. I do this daily and visualize*

myself eating from this tree. Then I watch my day unfold
to see what Wisdom comes to me.

Orion is the God of Divine Love. He governs the activity of Divine
Love. It is through this power of love that the human form is
able to hold together.

> *I call upon this aspect of Divine Love each day. I give*
> *thanks to all of my body elementals for having such love*
> *for me. They come together and work in tandem to provide*
> *me with the best vehicle possible for me to use while being*
> *upon the Earth. I also extend this love to all of Nature and*
> *humanity.*

Purity maintains the Divine perfect picture of purity for the Earth.
He helps all who live upon the planet reach their desired state of
purity within.

> *I have learned that Purity is the acceptance of all that*
> *I am. So when I work with Purity, I do so from a place*
> *of loving everything—no matter what I have or have not*
> *done. This is how I have been taught to work with the God*
> *Purity. I am told to accept all of me; it is what purity is*
> *for; it is all God.*

Cyclopea (also known as **Vesta**) is the God of Concentration and
Consecration. He oversees sight, sound (music), and speech.

> *When I enlist the help of the God Vesta to assist me, I do*
> *so through asking that my thoughts stay on track and that*

I do not become scattered. I have learned that to manifest your desires, you must stay focused on what you want to create. I then ask that my speech be clear and honoring always of myself and those around me. This does not mean perfection, for I know from the teachings of Purity and Jeshua that it is all about loving myself in each moment.

Peace brings peace and tranquility to this planet and to the hearts of humanity.

When I enlist the help of Peace, I do so through asking that my heart stay out of the old scripts of judging. I have learned that peace comes to you when you stay centered in all that you are. Like Jeshua says, we need to stay in the center of the compass.

Arcturus is the God of Freedom. He works with all prayers that are offered. He helps direct the Violet Ray to the Earth. The Violet Ray is energy that helps transmute discord. St. Germain is Keeper of the Violet Ray. Arcturus helps humankind to reconnect to their Divine Self.

I work with St. Germain daily. I know he directs the use of the Violet energy here upon the Earth. Each day I call him forth and sit in the violet energy for 20 minutes while doing the rest of my meditation work. I ask that this loving energy transmute all that does not belong there inside of me. This is a very loving and compassionate energy and can also be used to help transmute the energy of your DNA.

Archangels are the main angels, the angels of the second Highest order.

** **Chohans** have been human and have reached their own state of perfection. Once they ascend from the Earth plane, they have the opportunity to serve if they so choose. If they stay and help, they are given the title of *Chohan*. Their work is to help humanity understand the *Laws of Life*. They are more closely connected to humanity than any other off-planetary Being. (Read example of this in SIDEBARS.)

Guardians are protectors of the Earth plane. The dolphins, whales, and Mer people are guardians and have been here for a very long time helping to protect the Earth.

Elementals are the fundamental building blocks through which nature is created. You have the Gnomes (Earth elementals), Undines (water elementals), Sylphs (air elementals), and Salamanders (fire elementals).

Divas are nature spirits that live in the same reality as humans.

Angels, Seraphim, & Cherubim are all part of the Angelic Hosts of Heaven. They serve the Earth silently. They are loving Beings that grow through their service. Most of their work is through sharing their Light and love with humanity.

9

THE VALUE OF SILENCE

Hello once again, my Beloveds; it is always a heartwarming experience when the heart of humanity connects together with that of the Heavens. Even though you may be small in numbers, you are mighty in the Heavens. As you get *ah-ha's* and you receive understanding, the information is carried into the collective for all to take part in.

This chapter's subject matter is *Silence*. There are many things that come to mind when you think of Silence. There is the quiet silence that occurs when you pray and are waiting for the answer to come. There is the silence in the Heavens as we watch what is occurring upon the Earth. One such being is called the *Silent Watcher* who watches the progression of the planet and those upon it without interfering, much like you watch your child when they are asleep. There is Silence after your children have played loud music and then have turned it off. You say, *ah, the Silence!* There is Silence when you go to sleep at night. There is the silence that follows when you have partaken in something that is so profound that there are no words or thoughts so you just sit in silence. There is the silence you feel when you have connected with the Heavens and are in total peace within and silence. There is the silence of the great void. Whether you are speaking of the Heavens or events on Earth, there are many different types of Silence to experience in both.

However, the *Silence* I have chosen to speak about at this time is that of the *Great Silence*. I will give you a meditation in a

112

moment so that you can experience it, but first, I wish to talk about it. Beloveds, no greater place could one go to in his/her life than to step into the *Well of Great Silence.* Within that Well, all knowledge, all understanding is there for you to drink from.

This Silence we will be journeying within is a beautiful field of peace—beyond words—a pure energy. It is composed of pure Light. It feels thick because it is filled with so many particles of Light and love that it clings to you. (It may remind you of a light fog. Fog can be dense, as people who live on the west coast of America and in the British Isles will attest to. One can barely make out the headlights of oncoming cars. (Pure Light can be blinding also.)

As you journey into the pureness of the Light, there is nothing but love within this energy field. It is silent, but not as you know it upon the Earth where there is deafening of the ears. (An example of that would to be deep within a dark cave.) The silence I am referring to is the silence of your own soul—the silence of the Father's immense love and beauty.

This silence is what you all are working toward bringing into your own souls. The Channel (Cynthia) in her own humorous way, talks about her brain being *off-line.* In a sense, she is going off-line so more of this silence can be embodied within her while she is living upon the Earth plane. This will become part of the experience in the New World.

It will be built through the desires of the heart in that moment. Think of it like this—to be in the moment with no worry, knowing each and everything that arrives is Divinely orchestrated. You would know all your needs are being taken care of. What would it be like to be that present for yourself? When your mind is not in conflict with you, doing all of the *what if's* or *oh no's,* you are then living in this kind of present moment silence. Shortly I am going to lead you through a meditation that will help you embody this type of experience—that of the great silence where you are totally present for yourself.

Scan your body right now and detect how much peace and silence there is within you right now. Some people hold more silent and peaceful energy than others, depending on their degree of mastery. As you become more capable of holding more of the Light, the physical body will require less and less noise in its environment. People who live alone and are used to the silence are capable of doing this more easily.

However, the mission here is to learn to do it while being in the presence of others. This is what I did, my Beloveds. I held this energy of silence and peace while multitudes of people were around me. Currently upon the Earth, only about 10% of this energy of Light and love is held in the physical form. The rest is held within the energy field of the Father, of which you are a part, waiting for your participation.

This is accomplished through your partaking of your own type of devotional practices each day. However, as more Light comes into the Earth and more of you awaken, you will then change your Light quota by allowing more of it inside of you. Thus you become the living expression of Father in His fullness—that of love, Light and profound silence-filled peace while being in human form. You refer to this dynamic as *obtaining your Light bodies.*

You can enter into this energy field through the Great Central Sun. One way to do this is to just follow your own silver cord (through visualization) into the Great Silence located past your physical sun. Your cord knows the way; so do not worry; you will not get lost. Once there you will go into this place of great Silence and be able to feel this immense Light that I have spoken of. It is not the kind of

Light that you think of that shines in the outward world, but Light within your inner-self. It shines brightly as you connect in and yet there is still darkness, for it is all the same—unified. Here you will experience the great void of the Silence.

If humanity could understood how to utilize this Light, you could re-grow your limbs if need be. Each person has within his/her body this kind of Light. You often have heard of the *phantom limb* where you still could feel the missing part after it had been removed. That is because there is still a *signature pattern of Light* that holds the imprint of that limb. Your Divine Blueprint is very much present even though the physical part(s) may not be present (2013).

In time, you will know how to pull that Light from within, send it to wherever a limb is missing and re-grow the missing part. Or, perhaps you have had organs that have been removed due to various difficulties. You will be able to re-grow organs also—whatever is needed.

Through spending time each day sitting in meditation with this great energy Source, you start to become more like this energy—drinking in this Light. You are in a very rapid growth period that started in 2010 and will continue on. You are preparing yourselves to do your new mission here on the Earth. Many of you are feeling a bit agitated, or feeling there is a need to move more quickly. And yet what it is you want to do—and you do not even know what that is—has not yet manifested. It is called the *Divine Timing* and therefore, you must wait until it arrives for you.

There is this push within you to connect more with the Great Silence—this pure Light. It is a little different from what you thought of as Silence, but nonetheless it is that Silence of which I am speaking. You have another type of Silence/Light as you go into meditation which can be viewed as a smaller Ray of Light, the I AM.

As you connect with your Christ-Self, you are being Christ-ed through this action. The Silence of the I AM is a little bit different than that of the Great Silence. As you connect with the Great Central Sun's Silence, there is an intensity of Light. Beyond that, there is another Silence, but I will not venture there for now. The energy you will be putting forth upon the Earth comes from your Christ-Self, your Higher-Self—your I AM Presence—and is fed by the Greater Presence which is the Great Central Sun.

Now I will lead you through a meditation: *Take in a deep breath and then exhale.* (The entrance point to the Silence is not in the physical heart, the front part of your heart, but it is in the sacred heart that is located between both shoulder blades in your back.)

Find your entry point there and move with your consciousness into the sacred area. Some of you may see an altar; others may see a sacred flame burning which represents the tri-fold flame. Make yourself comfortable within this energy. Follow the visualization, but do not think of anything as you read this and allow me to guide you into the Great Silence. (You can even make your own recording of the meditation and then play it back to yourself as often as you wish in order to take this journey.)

As you connect with your sacred heart, feel that energy now—peaceful and calm. In order to enter into the Great Silence, one must detach from the outward world—from emotional issues as well as the chattering of the mind. Those things must be left in the outer world. If you have difficulty detaching, you can always tell the chattering mind, *I will come back and listen to you in a little while, but right now I am going to take a different type of journey. So I am going to disengage from you, but know I will be back to retrieve you.* Sometimes the body parts are in need of reassuring that you will not be leaving them behind.

Now, *focus on the heart space, taking in deep breaths—inhale and exhale—and as you do this, put forth a call to your Christ-ed-Self—your I AM Presence. As you put forth that call, see a vibrational color of pink that you will send forth when you utter the words. When you do this you are sending love to your own I AM Presence. As you pave that way with your love, you are making a call for your Presence to support you in joining the Silence.*

Side note: If you are having difficulty with the mind chatter mentally, see yourself taking your hand and pulling the left and right hemispheres apart. Start at the base of your neck. Pull the left part away and then the right part away, leaving the center part of your brain open to experience the void. Move your hand up a bit more and take another part of the left hemisphere and pull it away and repeat that same action for the right. It is similar to peeling away segments of an orange. All will be put back at the end, so do not worry. Move along the center line of your head until you come to your forehead. Picture this psychically and see a huge strip going down the center of your head. This helps you to enter into the Silence.

With the *call* having been made, I will intensify the energy. *You will begin mentally traveling up this beautiful energy cord—up to your Christ-ed-Self, up to your I AM Presence—and now moving into the Great Central Sun. As you move into the Great Central Sun, it is void of sound. There is only the Silence. Experience this energy. With your inward eyes, look around within this Silence and see the beauty of this Light that burns bright and yet does not burn your eyes. It bathes you in unconditional love.* This Light and love is all that is, my brothers and sisters. Nothing else exists. From this place, miracles occur; from this place of the Great Void of the Silence all healing takes place.

When you have completed your time sitting in the Great Silence and are ready to come back out, follow the energy cord back to your body. Once fully back in the body, put the left and right hemispheres of the brain back together (if you have done that part of the meditation.) Remember to put them back together in the same manner from which you had pulled them apart. Do not hurry this process.

When I was upon the Earth, I utilized this energy to bring forth healing. For those of you who do **Reiki** and other types of healing, you are using the same kind of energy flow from the Father. The deeper you are able to let go when performing these healings, the more you will be able to merge with the Great Silence. When body work is done, the cells receive this Light—this energy—with more purity and with more love. When you are detached and allow the flow to come through, there is not anything the cells can do but match that vibration. It is a remembrance within the cells that help them to recall what a healthy state of being is all about. From this place of stillness, you can call forth all of your own desires in life as well. For you will remember what it is like to be free of struggle and to just be!

If you wanted protection for your physical body, you would summon this same energy that I have been speaking of in this way: *I ask that the Lord God of my I AM Presence bring forth the Herculean strength of protection to be placed around me and within me. I ask for the wisdom, the love, the energy of healing for my body and mind as well. I thank you, Amen.* If you are having difficulties in a relationship with a relative, a friend, or in the work place, you would summon the Forgiveness Prayer from this place of Silence as well.

I call upon the Forgiveness Prayer; I ask that it be activated now; I call upon the Violet Flame to be activated, to transmute the disqualified energy between me and (supply the name). As that energy is purified and cleansed, I ask that a blessing be given to that person and that a healing occur between the two of us.

Now, Beloveds, I encourage you to journey back here any time that you desire and partake of this great Silence as many times as you like. When you are done being in the Silence, bring your consciousness back down the energy cord and see yourself back in your body once again. This is an inward journey. You cannot connect into that Great Silence *except* through your inward world. That is why you entered through your sacred heart.

The Great Silence is where you make your decrees. You enter first through the Christ-Self, which is the grid system. (Christ is a Principle; it does not mean me. But I did establish the Principle upon the Earth plane when I came—that is why I came—the purpose was to activate the Principle through the DNA.) As you travel into this place within yourself, you connect in with the beauty that is here.

If you wish to manifest something, you summon the energy forth three times as to what you desire. Then you give thanks three times. You also must charge the energy of what it is you desire at least once in every 24-hour cycle until you become perfected in living in the higher states of being. The Silence is void of any emotional charge as far as drama, but it is activated—brought into power—through the **emotional** center of desire. **The key here is the DNA, which means Desire—Need—Attraction.**

You can also picture it highlighted in a brilliant white Light. Frame it in your mind so that it shines brightly. You saw the brilliant Light of the Great Silence so use this energy to frame your own desires. Feel within you your desire, need, and then the magnetic attraction for it to come to you. You can take that Light energy and put it around what you are focusing on and make it flash. This helps bring it to you even faster. Remember on your TV how they flash things or better yet on the Internet. The creators know this principle helps the mind to pick up what it is seeing and thus brings it to you.

This puts that creation part of you into hyper-drive. That energy basically is then burned into the imprint of your mind which helps bring the object of your desire into manifestation.

It is important to charge the energy every 24 hours because you have yet to master yourself, as I said earlier. Your mind can drop too easily back into negative thoughts and thus cloud over what you have wanted to create. (Like the lampshade example I spoke of earlier.) Consequently, it is easy to switch back into the negativity of your critical side, saying that *there is no way you are going to get what you desire.*

When you charge it every 24 hours, you send forth that energy and your mind then switches from its negative thinking cycle back into its affirmative, positive side. This is how the entrainment starts to take place. If you do not do the recharging every 24 hours, your I AM Presence—first it is your Christ-ed-Self, then your Godhood, the greater Presence, the I AM—retreats from the Earth desire, need, and attraction and thus becomes negative once again.

It is never about the Christ-Self—your I AM—leaving you, but this Higher Aspect must pull back at this point in time. What you have been working to achieve could bring the opposite to you if the full Power stayed connected into you. In other words, you have moved outside of the flow of the Universe. You have let that flow move back into the fears of the world. Therefore, you no longer are in the Beam of Light.

Consequently, your I AM moves up and waits for you to realign yourself. By re-charging your desire every 24 hours, it burns the image into your mind so intensely that the negative part of yourself does not have a chance to take it away—self-sabotage.

When you decree something, you state: *In the name of the Lord Jesus Christ, I call upon my I AM Presence.* **The reason you include**

my name is because I am the one who brought forth the Christ-ed understanding of the DNA. You still have not mastered fully the joining with your Christ-Self. I say that as a general statement for the masses, for some of you have mastered this and more will do this in the near future. There will come a point when you will no longer have to decree in that way in the New World. But for now you do, for I AM the Way—I AM the Way-Shower—and I help you make that connection.

Many of you have seen the movie *The Matrix*. In that movie, when you wanted to plug into the old reality, there was an insert plugged into you and into the denseness. Consequently, you saw and felt the other paradigm as though it were real.

As you move away from the old paradigm, you are going to see the world differently from the way you could see the world before. You will see the Light and the love of the planet. You will see in ways that you have never seen before. You will experience all that is through the heart. You will experience the love of that person on a very soul-felt level. You will not experience the density because they have been un-plugged—just like in the Matrix movie.

This is what is happening, Beloveds. You are being un-plugged from the reality that you saw before. Those people that you have seen in the old way you will now see through the eyes of love. As you see people differently, you are going to mirror to them a different way to see themselves. That is how the healing on the planet takes place.

They have not been seen with those eyes before; they have been seen with critical eyes. Consequently, you are going to be the physical angels upon the Earth, holding the Light and viewing people as their true essence of whom it is they are. As you see them with this intensity of love and Light, they cannot help but see it reflected back and make those internal shifts.

So many of you have taken the journey which is not always the easiest—we do understand that, Beloveds—to lay that template, to bring that Light energy into yourself so it can be reflected back out. This is why your bodies are going through so much—the cells moving, being unwired and rewired at the same time, like you have been plugged into a Light socket here upon the Earth. It is because you have a different voltage being wired into you that you can tolerate a stronger current.

Lightworkers have not had a great deal of support in the past. You have felt you are really the *Lone Ranger*, although the Heavens have supported you. As you journey into the three-fold flame in your sacred heart and connect with that Light, there is a magnetic energy that takes place. As the Lightworkers join hands in the Upper Realms, you will pull through such intensity of that Silence of the Great Void that your bodies will become similar to the Las Vegas lights—and even much brighter than that! This is an analogy of how bright you will shine: As you shine that bright, then the New World will be built upon these levels. Everyone who not yet has joined these levels will be looking around and exclaiming, *how did you get there? How did you do that?* You will become the teacher and will share how you did it. Thus you will show them the way to the *elevators*—and they will be lifted up so all can return Home once again to LOVE. (2013)

You will become the Lighthouse for those ships that are lost upon the *Sea of Illusion;* so have faith, my Beloveds in what you have chosen to do in service for the Father.

Manifestation will speed up; that is what this next level is all about. Because you are Light and are letting in more Light and using energy differently, the energy is utilized in *manifestation*, whether it is positive or negative. Understand that everyone on the planet is ascending to some level. I am referring to an intensity level that can only be achieved, Beloveds, as you master your way of thinking. Thereby, your Christ-Self will not allow entrance into this great ability to pull energy if you are in negativity for the harm that you could do to so many.

When you begin to align, there is a rush of energy that comes toward you, for anything that you have manifested in any lifetime will find its way back to you. **There is a signature pattern that all energy has;** it knows its maker. It is not to be afraid of that dynamic, but to understand what it is you do—so you do not suffer for all of the energy that perhaps was not the most benevolent. Your journey upon the Earth has been to experience life in all its forms—benevolent, as well as malevolent. Therefore, do not judge the lifetimes when you were not in your heart and not benevolent.

What you do is to call forth the alignment of your Christ-Self; you move into the Great Silence, the Great Void. You make your call from that position to bring forth the Forgiveness Prayer, the transmuting Violet Flame for all Beings that you have ever harmed; you ask that the energy be transmuted and returned to Source. Ask that all of those individuals through all of the dimensions and time frames be blessed as that energy is removed.

Can you imagine the shift upon the Earth if all you Beloveds made that call for five days? It is because you are calling the alignment of your Christ-Self forth for the healing in your DNA of all the malevolent things **you** have ever done—all the abuse that has ever existed and thus has influenced many individuals. You are asking that all of that be undone—the malevolence. You are asking it to be transmuted and then asking that those people be blessed. This would affect thousands of individuals as the energy that they have been plowing through is suddenly lifted from their shoulders and blessings are brought to them.

Therefore, in the alignment with your Christ-Self, as you put out that call that the Forgiveness Prayer be activated and the energy be transmuted, and if you run into any difficulties with anybody as you go throughout the day, realize it is because of the energy field that is present **within** you. You call forth that shift in energy and then there will be a change there. It is a beautiful way to bring forth a greater healing upon the planet.

Your world is going to change very rapidly, Beloveds. The next two years (2010-2012) will be equivalent to a thousand or more years upon the planet in evolution. That is how quickly it is going to shift, because the New World is being created as you read these pages. Think about where you are today, just as a marker of where you were last year; you do not even resemble the same person. You are going to see the outward world with different eyes. Then you will change yet again as you enter into 2013. By the end of 2013, you will not look or act the same and so on until all are once again residing in total peace.

Now more than ever (because of the new vibrations) through using the Forgiveness Prayer, you will release rapidly that which will help the planet, as well as yourselves, to ascend quickly—helping to remove the malevolent energy that has been. There are those who have preceded you and have paved the way for you now through using this Prayer.

I have mentioned *mirrors* on more than one occasion. Therefore, let's take a deeper look into this subject matter, my Beloveds. Your inward world is all there is; this is where truth exists. That is where your Godhood and your connection to the Heavens is. The Light of who you are can only be found in the inner world. **Everything**

outside of you is false. It is a reflection of what your inward-self has chosen to create in the outward world. Your outward world is created through thoughts, intention, and desire.

If you think you are not loveable, your reflection outwardly will be that you pull people *to you who cannot love you.* If you think inwardly that you are abandoned, then your reflection will be that *everyone abandons me.* People get lost in the outward reflection of their issues; in this case we are talking about *abandonment*, rather than realizing that it is a personal issue within. Here is what your Higher-Self may be saying as to why this is being created. *I am going to shine my abandonment issues outwardly so that I can see what I have yet to heal within me. It has been my belief structure about life for so long that now I need to get this healed.* (You are probably angry at God as well.)

If you go deeper than the Father, knowing you are the Creator of your reality, ultimately what you are angry at is you! You forgot your Godhood; you forgot that you came from this Spark of Source. You instead believed what is outside of yourself. You believe the mirrors are real instead of a reflection. My Beloveds, mirrors one day will shatter as each of you take accountability for **you**. You will no longer need others to play a role for you in your own self-designed play. This is what is so exciting about the New World. The only thing that will be left is pure love; so you will not need the mirrors any more, for you have become the essence of love within yourself. (2013)

However, until that time arrives, mirrors will become more real to you until you get so tired of them that you are thus willing to look at life differently. The mental picture I will use for you is the House of Mirrors at a Carnival where the mirrors are all distorted. Your personal mirrors in the past have not been all that clear, for it could take five lifetimes (as an example) to clear a particular mirror. Now mirrors are instantaneous. It used to be the mirror was so distorted you could not even tell it was you (like at a Carnival) being reflected back at you. Now the mirrors are clear and precise—it is you! You will be forced to see the truth of your own reflection and you have progressed enough in your own evolution to understand how this works and why.

Let us use this vehicle, Cynthia, as an example. The mirror is that I, Jeshua, come through her to speak about God's Energy. However, that is not only the subject matter for today. What I also am doing is mirroring to you that **you** are Sparks of God and who you are really is a Being of Llove. I am reflecting this to you, as well as to Cynthia, in the internal realms. When love is reflected back to you, you can't help but shift your energy. Your true nature knows that you are love; so you start to remember when it is reflected back to you. (2013)

If you want love, you become love; if you want to be honored you must honor yourself. It is not about anyone else. Your relationships in the future will only reflect love. This will be amazing to watch in your world when everyone starts to awaken to who they are. As you have been working out karma through mirrors, the relationships in the future are switching from karma to dharma (*to hold and support—the Cosmic order that applies to all Beings*). Your relationships will start moving to a completely different level in their evolution.

Each person will start to live his/her truth, which may not be your truth, but it does not matter for all truths are correct. There are many roads back to Father. In other words, the internal world as well as the external world is ignited through the DNA. One dynamic is done through triggering mirrors to ignite the DNA in order to view your outer world, while the other is done through igniting the DNA internally by your deciding how you want to love and honor yourself—which ultimately was triggered through the mirrors of *remembrance.* The more humanity connects inwardly, the sooner mirrors will shatter for you and all will become Beings of Light and love. Those of us in the Heavens, like me, will no longer need to hold the Christ Flame because **you** will become the Christ within yourself.

That is why I come to you now in this way, as opposed to the Scriptures of old. Sometimes I quote Scriptures as a cross-reference; however, it is time my teachings become more current for everyday life. How can you relate to me as a brother, not one on a pedestal but someone equal in love, if I quoted Scripture all the time? The Clergy quote my words through the use of Scriptures; however, it does nothing to let you know how powerful you are and how to gain that power for yourself! These are now very different times, and you need more up-to-date teachings that you can relate to. (2013)

When we go to join the Father, there is no *oh, you were Jesus.* We cannot say that anymore than I can say *oh you were King Tut; you were Buddha.* It is not the energy of the names and positions that are important; it is the essence of the love and the Light, and the service to Father.

My brothers and sisters, I want to remind you again, your cells are vital forces; they are energy circuits. As you drink in the energy and move into this Light of the Silence and see the brilliance of the Light there and call it forth so that it comes into each cell of your body, you will begin to bring about a shift within the cellular structure of your form. That is done through your intent; that is done through your desire and your feeling center (*heart*).

It is important when you make any call (to God, your I AM, the Masters, Angels, Guides) that you call from the heart center. If feelings are difficult for you, ask your I AM Presence to help charge you in the feeling center—to help bring those feelings forth. You can think of something that triggers the heartstrings to open while doing mental exercises that help warm you up. Perhaps there is an animal or a loved one that would help stir your heartstrings to open within. As you think about your loved one, that is when you insert the energy through making your call to the I AM. This will help this Light to come in to the cells.

When making these types of calls remember to drink plenty of pure water, for this will help hydrate you so you can contain within your cells this flow of energy.

I thank you my Beloveds for being here with me. There is always growth when hearts join together such as is occurring now.

I AM Jesus/Jeshua ben Joseph. (3-20-10 & 2013)

10-A

THE MANY FACES OF JOY

Joy has many aspects. We are birthed into joy. The mother gasps in her birth pains and then laughs in joy when her baby springs forth.

Throughout the ages, people have struggled in finding joy in their lives. Humanity really does not think of bringing joy into its life. It just happens; you do something and it is joyful, you think. However, do you create an incident that is joyful and then ever feel lack of joy? My Beloveds, you have the ability to bring joy into every waking moment of your life. Think back on the various things that you do. Going out in the early morning and hearing the birds call and watching the sun rise on the horizon—does that not bring you joy?

For those of you who love to walk and tromp through the forest, does **that** not bring you joy? There are areas in California known for its Redwood trees and its Sequoia trees. They are so majestic—so majestic. In the early 1930's or so, one tree was carved out so that the old Model T Ford could actually drive through it. That tree is still standing today. However, was there not joy and awe of being in a grove of trees, ancient beyond measure?

And yes, the people who desecrated that tree by carving it out did not know any better. However, they were taking joy in the fact that the tree was so large that they were able to do this—to drive through it—and not kill it. People would stand upright in the center of the tree and joyfully have their picture taken.

How about all of your sports—the joy you experience when your favorite team wins is so evident in the way people celebrate afterwards.

In ancient times, joy was found, elation was found among the warriors who outwitted their enemies and won their battles. That was joy for them in that era. Therefore, you see, My Beloveds, joy can be experienced even in destructiveness.

There has been much written on joy. It is becoming known that without joy in one's life, one is no more than a puppet on a string being manipulated by its circumstances. People may ask, *was there always joy on the Earth? Was this something we brought in or was this something that the Gods in the Heavens gave to us?* It is an energy band from the Gods that humanity taps into. It is always available. It can be fleeting, but it is always there.

Now some of your activities may bring you a moment's pleasure. However, even in that moment there can be joy. For you women, how many times have you come home from a shopping spree and have taken delight and joy in your new outfit and/or your new pair of shoes? But it can be fleeting, as I have said. In other words, you have tapped into joy just momentarily, for when you wear your shoes, perhaps you find that your feet hurt. The shoes may look beautiful, but walking in them is not that pleasurable and the joy slips away.

However, joy has not gone anywhere; it is merely your outlook, for you can take joy in the fact that you allowed yourself that moment of pleasure. You allowed yourself to spend some hard-earned money in order to experience this joy.

When the Gods decided to bring new energies to this new Earth that they had created, they thought of the different attributes that humanity would need in order to have a wonderful life experience. And do not forget that you are one of those Gods. Therefore,

you wanted to have a wonderful experience. So you thought to yourselves, *what would bring me happiness; what would bring me great pleasure so that I would experience joy?*

So you see, there are aspects of joy. The Gods thought of all the energy bands that they could bring to Earth that would help them experience life in its fullness. Joy was one; Truth was another, and Forgiveness—which is one of the energies I brought on the planet—is another. Think of all of the attributes that you strive for, and they are usually from an energy band of some kind. These bands are available for you to tap into—to merge yourself into, to allow yourself to feel more deeply.

Those in a dark energy can also feel joy. They can feel joy as they harm another. They can feel joy when they have caused a disruption in someone's life. Those are darker faces that they have put joy on. In other words, joy is an energy band that you can tap into, but how you use it is up to you. You were given free will and therefore, it is up to you and your free will to choose your experience with joy, whether in a negative or positive way.

This Channel, Chako, was thinking about this assignment I had given her on channeling a chapter on *Joy* for our book. She was thinking how the different accomplishments of her three adult daughters have brought her such joy.

She is a senior, a grandmother, and a great grandmother. As she has watched her *girls*, as she calls them, emerge into their womanhood, they have brought her great joy as they reached the different pinnacles of their lives. She vividly remembers the joy that she felt in watching one of her daughters coming down the aisle to obtain her college degree. What joy she felt with her daughter Sandra's accomplishment—so joyous on that day. (Read SIDEBARS for memos on her other daughters.)

Therefore, you see when you experience joy with someone else and you are a part of their joy, it inspires you to go on yourself because you want the same experience that had brought them joy now to bring you joy. You want to feel the joy of that accomplishment also. Maybe your life had been so full up to a certain point that you had no time to go to college. Maybe you did not have the reserve money for the tuition. However, perhaps that has been freed up now so that you too can obtain your college degree and even to go on to graduate school if you wish.

Hence, joy can spawn off, or we can say that joy in another person can spawn off joy for someone else, becoming an incentive. When you are in your joy, you inspire others. It is catching (*smile*). You have just caught joy from someone else.

In the Spiritual realm, people who learn to channel are in joy, for it is joyous to be able to communicate with the Spirit world. Now this Channel is in joy every time we Masters come to her. I am Jesus the Christ. I am Jeshua ben Joseph, and when I gave her this assignment to write something about the *Faces of Joy*, she was somewhat hesitant, not because she would not honor my request but in the terms of *how will I do that? Will you help me, Jeshua?* She forgets sometimes that she is a conscious channel. She forgets sometimes—once a channel, always a channel. Your mind is forever connecting to the outside influences, connecting to the higher vibrations that make up your world and can bring great joy to the person who has made that connection.

There are many authors out there who are writing their books, completing their books, publishing their books, and therefore, feeling the joy of their accomplishment.

Dear Beloveds, almost anything you do, whether it is a task or an amusement or spiritual devotion, can bring you joy. Joy permeates the world. It is for you to tap into. Joy opens people's hearts. When you are in joy, your heart chakra is expanding. For those of you who do not have this information, you have your regular heart chakra and then you have your sacred heart chakra which is entered through the space between the shoulder blades in your back. When you are in that deep place, it holds no pain. That heart chakra is without pain. It is reserved for your experiences of joy. This is where you go when you are in your deepest spiritual experiences. You are in joy with the devotion of the Father.

Joy stretches your heart so that people like being around you, for you are optimistic. As you have experienced, there are people who are pessimistic. Everything can be a negative to them. Their cup is always half empty. But when you are in joy, dear friends, your cup is always running over. You are optimistic and you love life.

I realize, of course, that when you experience life, you experience it in all its facets. Therefore, you go through the life and death cycles. That is life; that is what you as a God wish to experience. You want to experience the fullness of life. So even though you may be holding a loved one, or be in a room with a loved one who is dying, you can bring joy in for that person who is passing over.

There is great joy at those times, although usually not talked about because the dying person may not be speaking. However, when you look upon his or her face, it is peaceful. If you only could see the other side as I can, you would see them cross over and see that they are in such joy because their trials and tribulations are over. They have had their experience. Their soul has grown. They have accomplished what they had set out to accomplish.

Now, of course, even in death—what you would call *death* and they would call *life*—you can have regrets. But that does not lessen the joy of the fact that you did it! You had your life experience and you have had your death. You are now back in the Heavenlies. You did it! Everyone is joyous and **you** are rejoicing. There are parties and reunions; everyone is in joy. You see that energy band of joy is everywhere and especially in the Heavenlies.

The many faces of joy—in the very beginning joy was brought forth by the Gods, by you, as I have been telling you in our book. Joy opens your hearts. There are so many aspects of joy. Joy broadens your outlook. If you are a pessimist, what a narrow life you must have, for you are sure as you climb your little hills of progress that over each hill is another depression, another trial that will be heavy and without joy. Those are such narrow perspectives. Joy stretches that out. It broadens your perspectives.

You may wish to jump up and down or to dance with joy. In the different cultures on your planet where people have brought a musical ear in with them, they dance; they dance in the street; they hip-hop and or break-dance in their joy.

There are places in America where people play the fiddle and then pass the hat around for your monetary appreciation. They take joy in the fact that they have entertained you; they take joy in the fact of their accomplishments, their talents—especially those dancers who can spin on the top of their heads, defying gravity.

Joy has so many aspects. It is throughout all of your experiences. It is for you to tap into; it is for you to acknowledge. And how many times have you said *oh, this has brought me such joy!* You are acknowledging that something triggered that energy band for you, and you are experiencing joy.

Think about the many faces of joy, my Beloveds. For some people, a gourmet meal brings joy. The gourmet cooks who created that meal are in great joy as they see you partake in their creation with such pleasure, as you smack your lips and moan and ooh and ahh over their culinary delights. *This tastes so good; look at the plate presentation; isn't it beautiful! Look at this spun sugar; isn't it gorgeous; look at the ice sculpture. Did you see the wedding cake? It actually looks like real creatures of the sea swimming on the surface.* What looks so delectable has taken the cooks hours to create, but they take such joy in their culinary art, for they are aware of pleasing not only their own pallet, but yours as well.

Think about the things you do in your life, the joy you feel in your accomplishments. Joy is almost tangible, for when someone around you is joyous—at a wedding—you feel joyous too. You are basking in their joy and they are sharing their joy.

Joy is such a part of your world, my Beloveds; it is a part of your world that you created—you, the Gods and Goddesses who have come to this Earth and tapped into the energy that you have created. This energy is all pervasive, and it affects every form on the planet. In the second part of this chapter, we will be addressing how joy affects your animals. Beloveds, always appreciate the fact that when you are experiencing joy and sharing it, your animals are experiencing joy, and they are mirroring your joy back to you. The domestic animals take such joy in being of service to humanity.

Beloveds, our discussion today has the purpose of awakening in you that you have a conscious choice to tap into the energy band of joy. It is for your consciousness to acknowledge, for these are choices. You have a choice to be in joy with the experience of your life or to view it in another way.

Joy is **always** available to you. Joy is there for the asking, the doing, the touching, and the being in joy. Joy and its many faces, dear ones, are yours. All you need to do is go to it, be it, and bask in it.

Be in joy, Beloveds. I AM Jesus/Jeshua.

10-B

FOR THE LOVE OF ANIMALS

Beloveds, I can well imagine that many of you—most of you even—have an animal now in your family or have had animals throughout your lifetime. These animals were **your** caretakers for as long as you would care for them!

Animals have always played a significant part for humanity, for they carry a Light within them. This Light comes from Father/Mother God just as the Light for souls does. Animals can be Lightworkers also for the Animal Kingdom. Each species carries Light that is a product of that particular animal. In other words, the Light for a rabbit will not be as powerful as the Light for a larger animal, such as a dog or the larger felines.

One animal could have more Light **and** spirituality—yes, there is spirituality among animals—and that animal can carry spirituality in a more dominant way than another animal. Just as there is more Light in a larger animal, there is a greater amount of spirituality in the larger species also. Humanity is not that far removed, therefore, for it too carries greater or lesser amounts of Light according to the development of the soul.

Consequently, that Lighted animal becomes the Way-shower for the other animals. There is a hierarchy of sorts among animals. The play *The Lion King* was not far off, showing the other animals bowing to the king's essence, or in recognizing the greater Light and wisdom of their king. There are Lightworkers among people who are Way-showers and the same holds true for animals. There can be Puppy-Way-showers; there can be Kitty-Cat Way-showers.

Now I know when we talk about animals, people want to discuss the Insect World or the Reptilian World. I will say that for this chapter, we will not be discussing those species at this time, for that is not my purpose.

I, Jeshua, have a great love for animals. It began actually on another planet. What would you say if I told you that my great love of animals came from the planet Venus? Isn't that an outrageous thought? Venus is known as the Goddess of Love. Everyone on that planet holds that vibration of Love, even the animals.

So what better planet to learn about love than from the beloved planet of Venus? Therefore, I fell in love with the animals. Some of the animals on planet Earth are a different species from what I had encountered on Venus. However, I will not go into that, for I wish to concentrate on this planet Earth.

When you go to a zoo, there is a whole array of animals that you can enjoy watching. Fortunately, your more modern zoos are giving acreage to the animals so they can roam in a more familiar type of habitat. But in your older zoos, the animals are in much grief and pain as they prowl about in their small cages.

Did you know that animals can suffer from these emotions? They have their emotional body just as humans do. You may be asking yourself, *what is an emotional body?* It is part of the different energy layers that surround a body, whether it is human or animal. As the human or the animal experiences any type of emotion—say fear—that energy (and remember that everything is energy) goes into the emotional field and resides there. It can be compounded time after time, building in intensity. Finally, if the field becomes too overloaded with that same energy of fear, it will create some type of illness in the body in order to dissipate some of the fear and alleviate the uncomfortable feeling. One could say that feelings go into the emotional field of humans **or** animals.

Probably the species that provides the closest example to love would be the felines—the kitty-cats—and the canine families—the dogs and puppies—who are so filled with love and joy. And since they feel their emotions so profoundly, there is a need to release the emotion that is predominant and taking over the body.

When you come home after you have been gone for just a short while, your greeting is as though your pets have not seen you for weeks. Their love knows no boundaries. If it is fear they are experiencing, they will cower and tremble in your presence.

These experiences have not always been so. Back in the beginning times of your Earth, the animals were larger and more ferocious. They chewed and gnawed on each other, either in territorial protection, or they simply just ate each other for a meal. The new Earth will eventually have no more of that. Animals will no longer be carnivorous. They will be vegetarians. However, all species will need to re-calibrate their whole digestive systems.

Sheep, for example, are used to grazing on grass or delectable leaves. And the bunny rabbits seem to eat anything that is green and colorful. However, sheep and rabbits will not eat meat. Their teeth are not made for that type of chewing, nor are their digestive systems able to digest meat. Therefore, put this in reverse, and the animals that are used to eating meat will find it difficult to just nibble on grasses and flowers and to digest all of that roughage.

There will be a period of time where the digestive tracts of the animals will need to change in order to make that transition from carnivorous to vegetarian. However, it will happen. Keep in mind that change is a slow progression and it will not happen overnight.

It may take a few generations for the old DNA to be replaced by the newer way of being.

Interestingly enough, when the animals make that food transition to vegetarian, it will make them gentler. If they no longer have to attack each other or other animals in order to survive by eating the meat, they can be more peaceful and just graze amongst each other. A wolf can graze alongside a little lamb and have absolutely no desire to attack it and make the lamb its meal. Those desires will dissipate, although it will take some time. However, that is the transition, the evolution, which will be taking place on the planet for your animals.

One of my first animal pets was a kitten, but a kitten of a wild animal—a lion cub. I found it when I was out walking the woods, hunting, for I ate meat back in that time. I found a cub whose mother had been killed and the cub was alone. I took it back to my home and adopted it. I loved it and it loved me back. You could use the term that I *tamed* it, but it was more that my love changed the DNA of that animal. I fed it what I had—fruits and wild vegetables. I cooked them to make them soft and fed them to the cub. What I was doing was changing the lion cub's desire for meat. I did not want it to grow up and look at me with a hungry eye for its next meal.

We had many wonderful years of companionship. It was a female cub and she grew and was my companion for many years. She also protected me so that when other predators saw us, they were not so inclined to come forth and engage us in any way. Through the years she did join a pride, but she came back every once in a while just to get her ears scratched or a bit of loving, shall we say. She was beautiful and I loved her dearly.

Therefore, you see, dear Beloveds, when I no longer desired to have these native experiences with the more predatory animals, I then came into different time periods where the animals were not as ferocious, although each species held its own personality. Each species acts in the way designated by its DNA coding—although there can be different temperaments within each species.

I noticed as the large mammoth disappeared and evolution advanced through millions of years, that as the animals became more important to humanity, the animals also became more domesticated. Animals have much to teach us. They teach us joy, adaptation. They seem to be able to adapt to their environment, not always with ease, but eventually they will settle down to a particular way of interacting with their family and/or neighbor.

They teach us relationship, companionship, loyalty in its particular form, and they teach us that no matter what is going on in our emotional life, our animal will always be there for us. They become mirrors for us, for they mirror their master's emotions and/or the family dynamics. In other words, you may be having a rocky relationship and not particularly be in peace with it; however, if you turn to your animal, **it** will be there for you, letting you know that it knows you are having difficulties.

Animals are extremely sensitive. They know when their keeper, their loving master, their loving mistress is having a stressful time. They will keep to your side and will try to sleep with you, or take naps with you. They have a playful part of themselves. They like nothing better than to tease you. They may hop onto your bed and nestle onto your pillow knowing they will get scolded. But they do it with such joy. They almost smile with their teeth gleaming. The joy that animals can bring to your life is amazing.

When a person is having an emotional melt down, your animal-pet will be there for you. This is usually for the cats and dogs, for they are the closest to having emotional ties to humans.

You can have other pets—pet turtles, pet lizards, pet fish—but you will not find the emotional attachment from those pets. You may be attached to them for they are interesting to look at, but there is no great love emanating **from** them. There is no great emotional support coming from them. However, you will find great emotional support with your dogs and cats, for that is in their job description.

There is a term you use depicting being able to communicate with animals. People say you are a *whisperer* when they recognize your ability. You can be a horse whisperer or a dog or cat whisperer. In other words, you are so tuned in to your animal that you intuitively sense what it is thinking and what it is saying back to you.

Many people who have a great love for their animals are *whisperers*. They just may not put that term to what they are doing. Little do they know that they are basically using their telepathic skills with their kitty or puppy.

Animals help to carry the energy of love, devotion, and faithfulness on the planet. We have said how animals are mirrors for you and therefore, they can help you develop compassion and love in your heart. You have only to go to a veterinarian clinic to see some of the emotions that are played out in front of you. When someone needs to bring an animal in for euthanasia, his/her grief is tremendous.

Love, Loyalty, Joy, Protectiveness are all Divine attributes stemming from your animals. They think of you as one they must guard and keep safe. It is a reverse role for you. They will love you unconditionally and teach **you** to love unconditionally. Give a baby animal to anyone who has what you would call a *hard heart* and watch that animal melt that person's heart.

Now of course, some people have particular preferences for either a puppy or a kitten. Many times the preference stems from a past life—what that person has experienced from a past incarnation. Maybe the person had a great love for a kitty-cat that died of old age. Now in this lifetime they still remember on a cellular level the pain and grief. Therefore, in this lifetime, they wish to have a dog, for they reason it will live longer than a cat and the person will not have to experience the pain of the pet's death—the separation—for many years, whether true or not.

Treat your pets with respect, for they are your great teachers. The Animal Kingdom is so wise, more than you will ever realize. Know that many times, your love or your repulsion of a certain animal most likely stems from previous lifetimes.

I know some people have a hard time believing they have had different lifetimes, let alone specific animals in that past period that would cause them to choose another type of pet during this lifetime. However, dear Beloveds, those are all belief systems that need to be reshuffled and transmuted and released. I can say unequivocally that you all have lived before! You have lived many times before.

That is one of the problems for the Christian religion, for they do not allow me to have that privilege. They want to think that I just arrived, taught my lessons, died on the cross and then arose from the dead and have lived in Heaven on the right-hand side of God ever since. Dear Beloveds, there is fallacy in that statement. I lived many lifetimes before the Jesus era. And when I did die and was with my Creator, I did not sit on a throne next to Him and just cogitate for eons of time. What a waste of energy for anyone to do that. The Heavenlies are very active, and there is great activity coming hither and yon for the many souls at all levels of evolution. Christians will not believe this; it is not in their reality.

There were specific reasons why I needed to experience life on Earth as many times as I did. I needed to learn about every species, everything about Earth if I were to be one to carry Light and Love for Earth's inhabitants. Would that not include the Animal Kingdom? Therefore, you can say that Jeshua or Jesus had pets in other lifetimes. We loved our pets and they brought us great joy.

This chapter conveys to you the love that I have had for animals and still do. I wrap my energy arms around the little animals that are making their transitions. People do not realize that as the animal or pet dies that it too is being greeted by the angels that guide these animals. Actually, they are from the Devic level, which includes your elementals, fairies, and elves. When a pet makes its transition to the other side, the angels there are quickly in attendance. Many animals die in fear, so that is one of the first dynamics to be transmuted—from fear to joy. Since animals have the capacity for emotions and there is a very fine line between the two worlds, they will see the angels as if they saw them in real life. To the animals, there is little change, except that the vision is clearer, the emotions are more acute.

When the fear has been alleviated, the joy can be more pronounced. The animals make their transition with joy, and they are complete. Many go back to their animal essence. Some linger and become part of Heaven, shall we say. When people die, do they not want to be greeted by their beloved pet? Indeed, for this also helps people make that transition more complete.

People ask me to please help their special little pet to make that transition. I gladly accept that assignment, for it gives me great pleasure to assist both people and animals to become joyful and at ease in their real World, the one of love and joy. I can relate to that; I do that; I love them.

We have our animals in Nirvana advancing and evolving just as the souls of humans are doing. This planet is going to change from violence to peace, to love. What better way to learn love than through your animals—through your animals that no longer desire to eat meat and/or each other. They can come and lie beside you. There will be no fear that you would be their next meal. If they ate you, they probably would become ill, for their digestive systems would not be able to handle meats any longer, as we have described.

Look at your animals, dear friends, with love and compassion. Do not, I beseech you, discipline them in a cruel fashion. Think of them as your furry friends, babies, and children. You ought never to take a baseball bat and strike a horse across its chest in your anger, although that has been done. You must never do that. You must never displace your anger at something and take it out on your animals. Horses are beautiful creatures. The more advanced ones have souls.

Many human souls put a thread of themselves into an animal in order to experience that energy. And conversely, your animal will put a thread of itself into you in order to experience people-energy. It becomes a two-way street. Always treat your animals as if they were another person of great Light living with you. It is a privilege to care for an animal.

You use the term you *own* that animal, but no one can really own another person; therefore, no one can really own an animal, either. That animal is its own Being. It has its own consciousness; its own type of learning; its own lesson plan, so to speak. It wants nothing more than to love you, to bring you joy, and to help you in your evolution as you are helping it advance in its development.

Watch over your animals, be happy, and give them plenty of water, warm places to lie in the winter months and cool places to lie in the summer months. Treat them as if they were your children. Treat them with love, for love and joy are what you will receive from them. They are some of the dearest creatures on your planet Earth. The larger of the species, say the cats—lions and tigers—are magnificent in their beauty and in their strength. It is amazing to behold them—the majesty of their species.

Everyone and every animal are evolving as the planet ascends; so shall these beautiful creatures that have been created by you ascend. Remember, *ye are Gods*—these magnificent creations are to be revered, to be honored.

Up to this point I have been talking about the animals that walk upon the land. What about the magnificent sea creatures in your oceans? You have all seen pictures of the seals sunning themselves on the rocks. You have seen the whales and dolphins jumping in your Sea Worlds. Those creatures are holding the Light for people. They are very wise and they carry the records for humanity. When you think of your land animals, your pussy cats and your puppies, know that the same type of joy and passion also exists in the sea animals—sweet little baby dolphins.

Let us leave the sea and think about the birds. Many people have birds as pets also. In Australia, there are flocks of wild parakeets, each a different color sitting in a row on the telephone lines—a picture postcard of exquisite beauty.

The Animal Kingdoms in the sky, on the ground and in the sea, dear Beloveds, are spectacular creations by *ye who are Gods*. Never forget that you are a Creator. Never forget that you helped to create these different species. You created them so that, in a way, you could have a mirror that would bring you joy, pleasure, and love.

Honor your animals as they honor you. Volunteer at animal shelters. Give the rescued animals love that is sorely missed by them, for it will help in their healing and allow them to find a new family with which to bond.

I AM Jeshua ben Joseph, or Jesus to those who have an attachment to that Biblical era.

11

THE VALUE OF GRATITUDE

Dear Beloveds, you know how I love metaphors, so I am going to use a metaphor to help you to understand the importance of *gratitude*.

We will speak today about a garden, a very special garden. Its caretakers created this garden, initially, in great love. Oh how they loved to garden! However, one day the caretakers of the garden had to leave their beautiful creation. As life happens, they had to move from their beloved home. This meant that their garden was going to be left on its own until someone else moved in and cared for it.

All that lived in the garden flourished through the love of the caretakers. Oh how happy the garden was; it had not known any other way to be, for all of its needs had always been provided for. The water came on a regular basis. The garden grew its produce; it was harvested on a regular schedule. The garden knew exactly what would happen each day because the caregivers took such good care of it and never missed a day attending it.

When it was time to plant a new crop, the soil was tilled and the new seedlings were taught by the other plants what would happen and what they could expect each day. Everyone was happy in this beautiful garden. They never had to give any thought to how they might be fed or watered, for they had never known anything else.

However, one day the garden went from a happy garden to the *Garden of Despair*. Soon after the owners, the caregivers of the garden, left, there was no one to water or feed them. Soon all in the garden began to grumble. No one knew what had really happened.

147

You could hear them saying to one another, *why did they leave us this way? We are all alone here! I am getting thirsty. I look at my leaves and they are beginning to wilt.* The discontent grew each day and soon it spread throughout the entire garden. The discord began to affect all of the little plants. No one was happy and their leaves and stems were no longer shiny and bright, but instead they were wilted and their heads hung low. They fell deeper and deeper into despair.

Then all of a sudden, a tiny little plant raised its head up out of the soil. It was a little different from the rest of the plants in the garden. It was a beautiful flower that was just beginning to come into its own. As it lifted its little head up, it looked around at all the other plants and exclaimed, *oh my, where am I?* It continued to stretch its limbs out and looked up at the sky. *Oh how beautiful everything is,* the little plant thought to itself.

Soon it couldn't help but attune to the grumblings in the Garden of Despair. But, not having been around as long as the other plants had been and being of a different variety, it was not able to understand what they were all grumbling about.

When the little flower began to get thirsty, it looked around and did not see anything happening. And so it thought, *what am I going to do? I feel a little thirsty today.* Then all of a sudden, it detected a little bit of water underneath its root system. So it stretched and it stretched until it grew a little bit of itself deeper into the soil. *Ah, there was the water.* It sucked the water all the way up into its leaves. It felt so grateful and basked in the beauty of having that little droplet of water.

The Garden of Despair continued with its grumbling, while this little flower continued to grow. Soon the Garden of Despair looked over at the little flower and said, what *are you doing? How is it that your leaves are so bright and shiny and our leaves are wilted and dying?* The little flower replied, *I do not know; I only know that there was a little bit of water right beneath my root. I reached down to it and sucked up the water. I am so grateful for that water.* The flower began to sing its song of gratefulness each and every day, for it knew that sooner or later another droplet of water would find its way to it.

The Garden of Despair watched and was cynical. There was no way that this could happen since within it were unresolved issues around its abandonment from the caregivers. In the Garden of Despair, there was only one way of being, and that was having all its needs taken care of. The Garden never had to figure out other ways of doing it.

The little flower did not have the same history. It only knew that it found a droplet of water and then sang songs of gratitude. One day as it was singing, a droplet of water fell from the Heavens—a droplet into the Garden of Despair. The little flower sang more and more of its gratitude for the little droplet of water that fell upon it, quenching its thirst.

Then there was a neighbor watering his yard, and a little tiny trickle came towards the beautiful little flower. Again, the flower sang its song of gratitude. Soon something began to change within the flower. A brilliant Light began to beam forth, and that was called *hope.* The little flower knew beyond any shadow of a doubt that its inner spirit was the way. And as it continued to feel gratitude, it began to shine hope out to the other flowers, for it knew it would become the most beautiful flower to ever exist.

Those in the Garden of Despair began to say to the little flower, *do you really think gratitude is what brought you the water?* And the little flower replied, *Watch me grow and decide for yourself.* Some of those within the Garden of Despair, as grumpy as they were, decided to succumb to gratitude while others stayed in their grumbling of despair. Now there were answers that they had not seen. Finally, the water began to spread throughout the Garden of Despair as more and more of the plants joined in gratitude with the little flower. Soon all of the plants realized that the answer to taking care of what they needed was to express gratitude.

My Beloveds, this is the story of your life. Just like the Garden of Despair, you have been fed a certain diet in your life. As you dropped into the densities in all of your lives, you were given a certain way of thinking how life had to be. You forgot about something you knew a very long time ago during Atlantis and Lemuria—all of your needs were provided for. As you dipped into the despair, like the Garden, you began to think that your needs were going to be provided by humanity's system of thinking. That is not how it works, Beloveds. That is not how you are provided for.

Hope—the seed of hope—is a beautiful Being that exists and is implanted in the heart of every human Being. What causes the seed of hope to spring to life is *gratitude*. It works with the Ascension flame—the ray. My Beloveds, through gratitude, you can bring forth your own Ascension; you can bring forth the answers to the difficulties within your lives. It is up to you to remember that all is energy. When you express gratitude, you touch directly into Father's Heart. Then Father responds back through your heart and provides you with hope that soon all will change. **The energy of gratitude moves the difficulties away within one's life.**

Think of a watering hose that has a crimp in it. The flow of energy is the water that flows through the hose and is stopped for a time being by some blockage. This is what has happened to you as you forgot how to access that flow of energy from Father. What you became was the Garden of Despair. So you blocked off your own watering hose from Father and moved into lack, just like the Garden. The truth is still inside of you, and it can be reactivated through gratitude.

When you have something occurring in your life that is very painful, hope tells you how to work through the lesson that is coming to you. I will use another example of a man who is waiting at the train station. As he sits there waiting for the train to come, he is afraid that he is going to miss his connection—a big business deal is in the works and he is worried that if he misses that connection, he will not have food to eat or be able to pay his rent.

Therefore, he paces back and forth on the platform of the train station, all upset. *How dare the train be late!* The more he paces, the more discord he creates. When the train does arrive, he is in such a foul mood. He gets aboard the train and it takes off. When he arrives to try to make his second connection, you guessed it—he has missed it.

Let us take another man who goes to the train station and is sitting there also waiting for the train. As he is waiting, he knows he has to be at a certain place at a certain hour to make his connection. He has just as much at stake as the previous man. However, he knows the art of moving energy. He knows that if he grumps, he will cause the kink in the hose—just like in the Garden of Despair.

Therefore, as he sits, he starts giving gratitude. *Thank you so much that there is a beautiful train that will take me to where I need to go. Thank you so much, for even if the train is late I will still be able to make my connection.* As he sits there giving gratitude, suddenly someone comes and sits down beside him. They begin to have a nice chat. They become very interested in what each one is doing in his chosen line of work. The man who had something to sell and was sitting there waiting for the train gives his business card to the person who approached him and sat down with him. They strike a business deal right there before boarding the train.

The train does arrive late, but it matters not. The salesman knows he has sent the energy of gratitude ahead, and all will be as it needs to be. As the train arrives at his location and he gets off, he is met by the businessperson who tells him, *All of a sudden, I had the idea to check the train's arrival time. I thought I had missed you. However, I was informed that the train was late. I am happy that I waited for you, as I really* wanted to *talk with you.* As they continued their conversation, the man makes another business deal.

My Beloveds, I have given you these examples, because in your own life it is important that you know that it is through *gratitude* that you move the energy. It is through gratitude that that seed within you, from the beautiful ray of *hope*, ignites and begins to blossom—just like the little flower. This sets you on the road to Ascension to discover your own Light, for you cannot ascend into the Higher Realms if you are living in the Garden of Despair. It requires you to live in a place of gratitude for all things in your life.

You come to the Earth plane to master the art of energy, to learn how to take what is labeled as *negative energy* and turn it into something to be grateful for. All lessons are teaching you to become a human-God. This is why I am so adamant about the subject of *gratitude*.

During the coming years, there will be many events that will occur. As these things occur, do not become the Garden of Despair. If it looks to be horrific in your eyes, perhaps **the event is meant to catapult humanity or you to open their/your heart.** If people open their hearts, they will begin to remember to be grateful for all that they have.

The Garden of Despair was not very grateful for continually being watered until all of a sudden the water was removed. As it learned its lesson from the little flower, then it understood the way to meet its needs was through gratitude—the art of gratitude. Be grateful and pray that humanity will be able to get the lesson(s) as quickly as possible and be grateful for your being upon the Earth. It is a beautiful gift to have life.

Be in gratitude during holiday seasons, for the seasons are about gratitude—about the New World's being created and living in love. The New World cannot be created until there is an awakening—a deeper awakening within the Garden of Despair—*humanity's* awakening to another way of seeing life.

The financial system will be impacted as the Ascension energies rev up. As it is impacted, share the teaching of gratitude over money with as many individuals that you can. What you say to yourself, whether someone takes you out to eat, or you find a penny on the ground, or whether you receive five extra dollars you did not expect, be in gratitude, for it matters not how it comes to you. The second it comes, switch it to gratitude. *Thank you, dear God, for this miracle of money. I give thanks for all my needs always being met.* By using these words, you have acted just as the little flower did. As you strengthen your ability to receive from the Heavens, it will increase your abundance exponentially upon the Earth.

Do this exercise from the place of gratitude for the little things in life and watch your life change, just like the little flower. Teach it to humanity—the story of the *Garden of Despair*. If you want to expand on this principle, call it forth for the miracles of the Heavens to open up. Ask that blessings/miracles un-numbered be poured out upon your head. Throughout the day, notice how many miracles you have—there is no limit to what you can create through the use of gratitude. Type or write out notes of the many miracles that have happened for you and put the notes around your home or office so you will be reminded not to forget to claim your miracles in each moment throughout the day. You will begin to collect so many miracles that you will have a hard time keeping count.

Soon you will touch the hearts of all around you who may be currently in the Garden of Despair, and you will be able to help them. But understand that just like the Garden, for those who can only experience life one way to suddenly not have it that way, the change will seem pretty dramatic to the Garden of Despair (humanity)—because it has not known it any other way. However, on the other hand, the little flower did not have that same rigid pattern. It was grateful to just be alive; it was grateful for the little bit of moisture it found beneath its root. It was grateful for the droplet that fell from the sky and soon it was being watered on a continuous basis. Humanity is the same way. The change does not have to be crippling, but humanity, since it has not known it to be another way, will most likely react in fear.

Gratitude is not always about being grateful for **things,** for there are other dynamics to be grateful for: your eyes, ears, hands, feet, life, your children, your pets and the list goes on and on. Help humanity to begin to see other was to rebuild its own Garden of Despair. Help people to understand they have within them the answers—like the little flower—for whatever it is that happens to them in their lives. Help them to understand the government is not the answer to all of their problems. Humanity must help humanity and give thanks to Father for showing the way.

Stay in gratitude, my Beloveds; it is now time.

Your loving brother, Jesus.

12

MY LOVE OF THE SEA

My dear brothers and sisters, you have only been given partial truths of who you really are and the origin of your roots. Have you ever wondered why so many of my miracles pertained to water? One of the first well-known miracles that I performed was that at the wedding of Cana. There was no wine for the guests, and my mother asked me to be of assistance. It is here that I turned water into wine so they could rejoice in the manner that was fitting for this time period. Or perhaps you will recall another well-known miracle when I sent my disciples ahead of me to cross the Sea of Galilee. I came to them when they were in fear of the storm. I did so by walking upon the turbulent waters they were afraid of. There are countless other stories you can find where I made water the highlight of a teaching.

My official duties to begin my ministry could not occur until I was first baptized, for I needed to be cleansed by Her Spirit (Holy Spirit). Look at John the Baptist, who came before me and how he insisted on baptism by total emersion. These are valuable clues left to help guide you to the real truth. Even your bodies are mostly water. It is my hope to stimulate you to begin questioning who you are and to dig just a little deeper into the truth of what I am going to say. Do your own research and draw your own conclusions when I have finished.

This planet is a watery world. In its original state, it did not have the land masses that you see today. There were times when this planet was covered in only water. It was pure and filled with a vibration of great peace and love, and it was out of this love that the Great Mother Earth volunteered to allow you to incarnate upon her. There were life forms that existed upon the Earth at this time.

These life forms lived in harmony with one another. One in particular is a Being you can call the *Dugald* (means *dark stranger*.) The Dugald bodies were similar to the human form; however, they had webbed feet and hands. Their faces were much like a cross between human and seal. This allowed them to swim in the water with ease. There were other forms of ocean life as well. However, the Dugalds are the ones that were the closest to what you could relate to today. They stayed on the planet for quite awhile and were here as the landmasses began to form.

Through the passage of time and the influence of the Dark Seed, the Earth became corrupted by the human ego. The Dugalds adapted for a while to the Earth's changes and were able to move upon the land as well as in the water. When upon the land, a sort of watery helmet protected their faces. Their skin had a built in water system to keep them moist for a certain number of hours. After that length of time, they had to return to the sea.

Eventually anger and corruption became too great for their gentle nature. They were removed so their gentleness could be protected until the time arrived when humanity chose peace once again. Before they were removed, all of nature worked in harmony and the waters held the energy of love and peace. A few of the Dugalds did volunteer to stay behind when others were removed. Those who stayed did so in an attempt to help the planet to hold the frequency of peace so that one day all could return. The Dugalds work in conjunction with the dolphins and whales and other cetaceans in the sea. They live at great depths in the water. Therefore, they have rarely been seen. When peace is established once again, all of their kind will return and help assist others to bring the purity of the oceans back. They have varied talents that will be greatly needed during the time of rebuilding which is soon to arrive.

During the time of Noah, the Earth was destroyed by water. The reason water was used to destroy the Earth is because of the story I just told you about the beginning of the Earth and how it held the energy of peace and great love. It was hoped that through destroying the Earth through the use of water, thus cleansing the DNA, humanity would remember who it was and where it came from. The water also helped to cleanse Mother Earth so she no longer held the energy of corruption and negative thoughts within her. (2013)

However, history shows you a very different outcome to this story. Humanity once again returned to the darkness. Know, my Beloveds that the **water molecule holds the secret to life**. Just take a glass of water in your hands and think of me while enlisting my help to lift the vibration of that glass of water. Now take that same glass of water, once the vibration has lifted (only takes a few moments with focused intention) and ask as you are drinking the water to know who you are.

Call upon your own I AM and say, *I now command myself to awaken and remember who I really am.* The molecules will activate your DNA to awaken you. Remember how I talked about baptism and why I needed to be baptized. It is all about renewing and remembering through the records that are held in the water. Every Being upon the planet is required to move through the watery realm gateway. This gateway is found in the Star System of Sirius. Many of you reading these words can remember and feel your deep and profound connection to these watery realms. You have this connection because, in fact, within your DNA, you are being triggered to remember your various faces. (2013)

If you are one who does not feel this same connection, that is because you were a land-dweller and even though you are comprised of water and came through the water gateway to get here, you have always been a land-dweller. Both forms of Beings existed upon the Earth—the human and those that lived within the waters at the same time. Many of the water Beings decided to become human, or land-dwellers. Some of you did this over a period of time, and some of you made the transition very quickly. The point here is that both existed. I am not referring to your evolution story. I am sharing with you that both forms of life existed, and there were interactions between the two.

The original teachers for the land-dwellers were those who came from the sea. Go back and study your Greek/Egyptian cultures. These are not myths; these are in fact truths that have been hidden from you. Some of you who lived in the waters made a decision to become human so that you would have a greater impact upon those in human form. However, with all of the ups and downs this Earth went through, many of you lost your way because of the influence of the dark ones. You became controlled by fear and bought into the stories of untruths.

The transition from living in the sea to land was harder than you had thought. Some of you today are not happy unless you are by water. This is why, for being by water helps you to remember your roots, and some of you even long to return to the ocean in the state that you once were. Reading this information no doubt will bring a deep sense of peace, while others of you may feel angry and feel like my words are nonsense.

I remind you what I said in the beginning about the different ways to look at a chair. From one view, you see one thing; from another vantage point, you see it differently. I am only adding another view for you to start considering—one that is not spoken of, but none-the-less is true. I am also making it known now that I, too, had a sea form. I was not always in the form of a man. I had many lives before I played the role of Jeshua ben Joseph—Jesus. You may know of some of them. However, you may not have known that **I was a dolphin**. Let me give you some other clues that you can research for yourselves if you do not believe me.

When I died upon the cross, these letters were inscribed, INRI. In English, this translates to "Jesus of Nazareth, King of the Jews." You will also see the acronym ICHTHYS, which also relates to me. It means *fish*. The fish became a secret symbol by which those who followed my teachings could identify one another. My mother Mary was of the sea also. This is a hidden truth, but if you research enough, you will uncover the truths that have been buried for much too long. The emblem that represents me, even to this day, is that of two fish which represent the Piscean Age. However, it also represents other truths pertaining to my lineage.

I often referred to my disciples as being *fishers of men*—another hidden clue. I could have as easily said *teachers of men*. All of my words were encoded with messages for those who would one day read between the lines and remember the truth. I had to speak in parables in order to give hidden messages, and within these messages there lay buried truths. This was done because the darkness was so great upon the Earth during that time. I knew the power of the spoken word and eventually, the written word. I knew one day these words would trigger the DNA for humanity to awaken. It is time to let go of the illusion. I remind you once again, remember the movie theatre analogy. I was one of many Ushers who came to show you the way out of the movie theatre.

Early Christians symbolized my death upon the cross by using a dolphin and a cross together. Ask yourself WHY this would have been done if they had not had direct knowledge of my true heritage? Constantine, however, forced the churches to accept only the cross and therefore, the dolphin was removed. Again, I ask you WHY and why were they afraid for this knowledge to be known?

Growing up, my mother often spoke to me about my roots from her side of the family. She knew that the time would come when I would need to better understand that I came from the sea as she had. I am not referring to this lifetime, as Mary and Jesus, but of our true heritage from the past. She was from Egyptian lineage and knew from her own upbringing how the Egyptians had honored the sea life. If you study how the pyramids and temples were made, you will find that they had water pathways built around them to enable the sea life to swim in. There were also miles and miles of underground waterways that were built as well. It is here that the dolphins would come and visit those upon the land and deliver the teachings from the Higher Realms. The dolphins maintained the Higher vibrations and knowledge. There is a lot of information available for you to uncover that will help bring more light to what I am saying, if you really want to know the truth.

Through my mother's sharing of these teachings, it helped prepare me for my journey—what is referred to as the *lost years*. My Grandmother Anna also talked to me openly about these things. I loved her dearly. She filled in pieces that my mother had not. My mother had my other siblings to attend to, so we were often interrupted during our talks and not able to finish some of her teachings. I was a very inquisitive young man, and it helped that my grandmother was always eager to share. She was an invaluable resource for me in understanding the true history of the planet and me.

I would often go to the sea to speak with the dolphins and whales in my lifetime as Jeshua (Jesus). They would communicate with me telepathically, and many times, I could be found in the water with them. I found them to be of great comfort to me during my times of soul searching. They helped me with the work I had come to do. They were wise and not easily influenced by the thought forms of those upon the land that were steeped in fear during these darkest of all times. They maintained their connection with the Higher wisdom of the Father and therefore, I found them a delight to be with. They also had a great sense of humor.

During my time in Egypt, I was taught more of the hidden secrets. I learned about the inner Earth (Agartha), and I went there many times during those years while being prepared for my ministry. I learned more about my past lives when I lived in the sea (more clarity on this a little later on). It delighted me so to remember the watery realms and my life as a dolphin. I was taught how to move inter-dimensionally at that time, which allowed me to visit other locations as well as my own past lives. It brings me great joy even now, as I bring these words to the pages of this book.

The watery realm exists in many different forms, or dimensional levels, not just the way you are used to seeing it in the 3rd and 4th dimensions. We lived in peace and harmony in these Upper Realms and would allow ourselves only to be seen when it came time for us to deliver our teachings to those upon the land. I say *us* because I was not the only teacher. There were others who offered teachings as well. The human Being during these times did not possess the Higher understanding of the Father. (In previous chapters, I spoke about the dark ones; this was the influence that was being felt during my time as Jesus.) Once our teachings were delivered in our dolphin forms, we went back to the sea.

We knew how to access the inner Earth and had no problem with changing locations upon a mere thought, if we so desired. We could also access multiple dimensions and therefore, we were not found swimming in the sea as you find your present-day dolphins. You may be wondering why we chose to keep our dolphin/sea life forms. We did so because it allowed us to keep the Higher vibration and thus maintain the purity of the teachings and not to become contaminated by the *fear* of those upon the land. Even today, there are times when I will appear to some who have this connection. I come not as the man, Jeshua, but in my dolphin state instead. However, they know I am Jeshua because they remember. I do this only with those who remember their connection to the sea and who would not be frightened by my dolphin appearance. So you can see now why I love the sea as well as you, my brothers and sisters, for I have lived in both arenas—land and sea.

The sea life today has taken on much of the destructive energy in order to help humanity make it through—so that they might emerge from this negativity. If not for the help of the sea, you would have perished long ago. The dolphins and the whales have held some very High vibrations and have been able to alter many of your destructive energies, which helped prevent wars that you would not have recovered from.

Some of the dolphins have even volunteered to be of service to the Navy. Why? The dolphins hope by helping the Navy, it would transmute the energy around humanity's warring nature. There is a saying on your Earth: *Keep your friends close, but keep your enemies even closer.* By being of help to the Navy, they have been able to work directly on the hearts of those who are using them. Things are not always what they seem. I am speaking of the dolphins and whales. However, there are many other forms of life that have helped as well. The seas are going through massive changes now, even as each one of you is. Much damage has been done to these wonderful waters and soon it will be necessary to clean them. Much of your sea life is dying and going to the next level to prepare the way for you in these Higher Realms, which are based on peace and love. You will need to change your ways to be in these Higher Realms. These Realms are filled with peace and love beyond your wildest comprehension.

It is my hope, my Beloveds, that you begin to do what is necessary inside yourselves to find this place of peace. Forgive yourselves; we in the Heavenly realms only have love for you. There is no judgment. What you are experiencing in your own lives is a reflection of what is inside of you—your belief systems and your own judgments. If you want a different life, then you must change *you.*

The channeling of this book helps to create a bridge between Christianity and Spirituality. You have a saying: *Don't throw the baby out with the bath water.* There is truth in everything, my Beloveds. How can you resolve duality if you have to make something/someone wrong in order for the other to be right? Yes, in some respects Christianity has done much to place fear within the consciousness of humanity. However, take that concept and look at it a little closer. If you did not judge yourself with fear, Christianity could not mirror that to you.

Now with that being said, I want to explain a little more about dimensions, time frames, and how I could have been a dolphin. To understand how this occurred, a greater picture must be painted first. As we proceed, you will begin to see that there really are no rights or wrongs. It is just that you have not received all of the information. So you have drawn your conclusions based on only a small piece of information—similar to looking at the chair I carved (metaphor) that I gave to you at the beginning of this book. There are multiple selves as well as multiple truths to the same question. I realize that upon the Earth today what I am saying about dimensions and other parts of your self are not yet widely accepted, along with the idea of reincarnation. You may be asking what the difference between the two is. The word reincarnation addresses linear time and moves in the 3D world forward and backwards. Multiple selves are the relationships between all dimensions and time frames. They exist outside of the 3D experience. Multiple Realms address all of the parts of you that are in existence outside of linear time and are present at the same time. (2013)

To help you better understand multiple realms and reincarnation, I will start with the metaphor of an onion. (If you want to use a real onion, go and get one now; otherwise visualize what I am saying.) Let's first start and peel away layers 1 & 2. We will start with the 3rd layer which represents your 3D world where you live. Now with that third layer of onion peeled away, look at the place where you began the peeling process. This will represent a past life—your first lifetime in the 3D world.

As you follow along the 3rd layer of the onion skin there are many cells that help to create that 3rd layer of the onion. Each cell we could say represents a passage of time. That 3rd layer of skin represents the passage of time when you were here upon the Earth living in the 3D world. Now let's say that you are coming to the end of these cycles and the teachings of the 3D existence have all been completed. All of the parts of you, or time-lines in the 3D world have now begun to integrate into you. This is called the *collapse of time-lines*. Remember you are the sum total of all the parts that have played the different roles in the 3D experience. You are graduating, dear ones. This is something to celebrate. It will happen to everyone eventually.

Now your I AM says once graduation is done that it is time to meet and start blending in or joining with the other parts of yourself that exist on other levels—or in this case other levels of the onion. So we will now move to the 4th or 5th layer of the onion (4thD or the 5thD). Your move into this level is dependent upon what you have asked for in your life. In this example, let's say you want to move to the 5thD. You are tired of all the violence and truly want to live where things just come to you with ease and grace and there is great love.

However, in order to skip 4D you would have had to learn the lessons of the 4thD. Perhaps your other self had completed its journey in 4D, so when you were ready to leave 3D, all you had to do is to blend with this part of you that had learned the lessons on the 4D realm. This blending and shifting can happen rather quickly. Perhaps it is during dreamtime, a daytime nap, or a momentary lapse of time where you thought you were just daydreaming. It can take as much time as needed to make sure you are capable of doing the blending process. *(It could also be that you need to spend some time here in the 4D realm until you have mastered more of it and then you can blend.)* You realize something just happened but you are not sure what.

For this example, let's say you can now move on into the 5th D and blend with this part of yourself that exists here in this dimension. However, this process is different. You know there is a lot to learn here, so you decide to hang out here for a while. Besides, the part of you that has been living in the 5th D has not completed his/her lessons and so you join together and now learn as one. (2013)

Through this merge with your other self, you are able to know what she has learned and you are brought up to date. Your vibrations are lifted and everything in the body that you once had has changed and continues on in your journey together. In these Upper Realms, time does not exist and therefore, all possibilities exist at the same time. So there is a very different learning curve to work with here.

You must slow down in this reality so you don't get lost with the faster movements of possibilities that are swirling around you. If you speed up and move as quickly as the energies are moving around you, you will literally go mad. Many of you are now moving into these Upper Realms of experiences. So you have to live in the present moment in order to exist here. There are many realms, my Beloveds, and each one brings new and different lessons. These are beautiful lessons and very different from those of the 3D world.

I am going to give you one more example of how to understand the jump from 3D to 5D. Using the analogy of a person driving down the highway, let us say he is looking for a place to eat. In the 3D world, a place to eat has already been built. In other words, the restaurant is in existence; you just have to decide what kind of food you want, the time you want to eat it and if you are eating in or out.

In the 5D reality, it would play out something like this: I am hungry. I want a place to eat that nurtures me. You look down the street and it is blank. Nothing is there because it has not yet been created. So you hold in your thoughts what you envision; this reality requires the use of strong intention. Suddenly, the place appears right down to the smallest detail. You get out of your car and go in and eat. Everything is to your satisfaction because you created it. Here you are the creator and the person experiencing this creation all at the same time. In the 3D reality, everything is already created and you have to decide what you want to take part in. Why? You might ask. Because you are becoming more your God-Self as you move up the spiral of Creation. (2013)

Going back to my life as a dolphin—I lived as Yeshua in a 3D reality when I was doing my teaching. However, in my life as a dolphin, there was a different vibrational reality through which I had more flexibility to move in and out of other realms. If you have a part of you in the 5D realm, that part can traverse downward. However, it can't move to the 6thD reality until all of the lessons are learned and that 6thD self is ready to merge with your 5D. Once the merging is done, then you can always move downward to where you have previously existed—that is if you really want to. This is why my dolphin-self could move all over the place and commune with me at any point in time. (2013)

One of my other selves is called *Sananda*. This is a Higher Aspect of me, Jeshua ben Joseph. When I say Higher Aspect, this is not better than, just different. Sananda had a different kind of work to do. However, it was still in serving the Creator/Father Energy. And, so it is with you, my Beloveds. You have other parts of self that serve and experience the various levels.

If we return to the onion, you could say Sananda is closer to the center core of the onion, whereas Yeshua was a layer of the onion further out. When I lived as Yeshua, I did call upon this other Aspect of myself, as well as the dolphin-self to help me, just as you may call upon your own Higher Self to help you in the life in which you now are living and reading this book.

Now let us talk a little more about my life as a dolphin and why I chose this as an experience. The ocean represents the Great Cosmic Waters. The day will come when your seas will return to a pure state once again. There is an energy that flows in the water that makes it easier to stay connected with the Father while learning how to be in form with the Mother. It is a great gift to have the Mother open and allow us to journey within Her Energy of love. (2013)

For me it was a necessary experience to have. This helped me learn how to embody love while being in a form. I would pull from this knowledge many times in my life as Jeshua ben Joseph. Dolphins are great Ambassadors and have the ability to open the hearts of everyone they come in contact with. I learned the art of loving unconditionally along with how to allow the Father's great love to flow continuously through me.

Many of you think it was written in stone that I would die on the cross—not so. Actually, it did not begin to formulate that way until it was realized how those in power had hardened their hearts and had begun to fear me, rather than open to me. During my time in the desert, I had to come to terms with many things within my own soul. I had to figure out what my next steps would be by going in and listening to my Father. The journey within is the only way to accomplish this. In order to ascend, every Being upon the Earth must take this deep inner journey. During the *lost years,* I was trained how to pull my essence from the physical body, should it become necessary. However, just like you, the mission was given but how I accomplished it was flexible.

I also experienced a life as a mer-person (merman), whale, and a few others. All experiences helped me develop talents that I would need in the future. Most of my ocean experiences were as dolphins and whales. As a dolphin, I learned about the art of Ambassadorship. The whales taught me about the history of the planet, as well as teaching me navigational skills through the depths of darkness.

This served me well when I became Jesus. Dolphins bring peace and excitement to everyone's heart. It is very hard to stay angry in their presence. They also have uncanny abilities where they can be in several places at the same time if they so choose. I wanted to learn how to do this while being embodied as a dolphin. The various forms of sea life help you learn different lessons. (2013)

One of the things I loved so much when I was a dolphin is how they fully give themselves permission to play. I would spend my days in my youth chasing my pod mates or they would chase me.

I learned a lot about how to stay balanced between work and play when I was a dolphin. I delighted in this experience and drew upon it many times in my human lives.

I am always and forever with each and every one of you. Call me forth and I will assist you, my Beloveds, in your own personal journey.

Romans 13:8 says to owe no one anything, except to love each other, for the one who loves another has fulfilled the law.

Let me add something to that scripture and create it as I would like it to be today . . .

Owe no one anything, except to love each other, no matter if you are human, animal, or of any other Earthly form. For the one who loves another and does not judge its form has fulfilled the Law of Unconditional Love. (2013)

Your Beloved Brother, Jeshua

(Authors' Reminder: when Yeshua is spelled with a Y, that depicts the spelling and the energy of that Biblical era. When his name is spelled with a J, it references present time.)

MY GREAT LOVE OF THE SEA

She is without form this great Mother of mine.
She teaches about Oneness and yet utters no words.
She shows us what love is through acceptance of all.
We know of Her great compassion as She holds us all.
She is always there to remind us that we are limitless.

Ah great Mother of mine, one day your story will be told
and those who are ready will weep tears of joy to know
You again as I have known You.
Your Dolphin Son (2013)

APPENDIX

MASTER YOURSELF

Scribe's Note: *As Heather Clarke, our editor, checked through the transmissions on Discord, she felt there was so much material on self-mastery that it could be a chapter in itself. If all the information for that chapter were left in, the chapter would be well over 30 pages long. Therefore, she extrapolated the teachings on self-mastery and suggested they be a separate chapter, which would increase the number of chapters from 12 to 13. Jeshua was using the sacred number of 12 and therefore did not want to change the energy of the book by having more than 12 chapters. This dilemma was resolved for me one morning upon awakening when the idea came into my head to put the following discourse in the Appendix. In this way, Beloveds, you have missed nothing of Jeshua's teachings!*

MASTER YOURSELF
Through Forgiving Yourself

Two thousand years ago I taught, as well as modeled, for humanity what it means to forgive. This is a teaching that has been carried down through the ages. Many have forgotten my teachings on *forgiveness* and have instead chosen to hold on to their pain. My mission as the over-seer for the Christ dispensation was to prepare humanity for the upcoming 2,000+ years, which will be brought forth during the cycle of freedom. Forgiveness must precede one's freedom. Your journey upon the Earth was never meant to be a struggle, my Beloveds, but because you have not fully understood what forgiveness does for your soul and for others, you have held onto your grudges. It is written in Heaven and upon the Earth that one must forgive in order to inherit the Kingdom of God.

Many times people do not offer forgiveness because they feel like the injustice done to them will be forgotten if they do not hold on to the memory. My Beloveds, the only one paying is you! All deeds done are recorded in the Book of Records and will be returned to the creator of those deeds, which means no one ascends until he/she is willing to be accountable for his/her own creations. Let us review **Matthew 18:21-22**—*Peter came to him and said, Lord, how oft shall my brother sin against me, and I forgave him? Till seven times? Jesus saith unto him, I say not unto thee, until seven times; but, until seventy times seven.*

My Beloveds, why would I say seventy times seven? Would you want the Father to limit the number of times **you** could be forgiven? In the bigger picture of Unity Consciousness, this person is you. Before your coming to Earth, it was agreed in the Heavens to bring to you through another what you are not willing to see within yourself. So when you forgive your brother, you are actually forgiving yourself. This is what the scripture really means. At the time this was brought forth, humanity could not understand the concept of others mirroring themselves **to** themselves. This is why the teaching 2,000+ years ago had to be taught differently.

Some of you are thinking about the people on the Earth who do unkind things to each other—like taking a life. You wonder how this could be. You would never murder someone. However, it is an out-picturing (mirror) of you, otherwise it would not be in your field of awareness. Using the example of killing, let me propose a few questions to you. If you say you would never kill another, I would ask you if you would ever be capable of killing yourself. If you say NO, you would not, then I ask you, are you killing yourself in other ways? I would say *consider your thoughts. Your thoughts kill the spirit within you.*

What kinds of words do you use in your inward dialogue with yourself? What are your food choices? Do you smoke? All of these are forms of killing as well, my Beloveds—a more painful and slower death—but do not think you are not doing the very act you just said you would not do. Therefore, you can see that the mirror of killing was being reflected back at you to get you to see what you are doing to yourself. All mirrors are things you are doing to others or that which you are doing unto yourself.

You say hurtful things to others that pierce their very soul. My Beloveds, this is worse than the killing of their physical body. Why, you ask? Because they must live and relive those words over and over again and die not once but millions of times by your hand. Consider the wounded children upon the Earth whose parents, out of their own pain, lash out at them. The children carry this in their soul the rest of their lives and even beyond. So you see, there are many ways of killing, and no one is exempt.

Let me give you one more example so that you might better understand *mirrors*. Let us say that you keep attracting people into your life who abuse you in one way or the other. You can't figure out why this keeps happening. The reason, my Beloveds, is because you are abusing **you.** If you love yourself (I do not speak of the way ego tells you to love.), you would never attract abusers. That is the way it works for those in the world.

Now some of you would say, *but Jeshua, were you not loving and yet you attracted abuse?* To that I would say *yes;* however, it was my mission. I came to show those in the church a different way of doing things. **My mission was to take unkind deeds and mirror Love back to humanity so that the world could start to change**. My Love for humanity was greater than the deed that had been done unto me. This example has served the world to this day in learning how to choose love instead of vengeance. I would also remind you that I came in with no karma; therefore, the mirror was not for me to see what I was not seeing, but instead to give a mirror to all of what *love* was.

I will guide you through the exercise of how to call upon the Forgiveness Prayer. It is not necessary from the Heavens' point of view, but it **is** necessary for you. Why? Because what keeps you bound is your own judgment about your actions—whether consciously or unconsciously. Father/Mother does not judge the experiences you have chosen. However, as long as you are judging yourself, there must be a way for you to find your own forgiveness within and that can only come about through *accountability*. This is why this Prayer was created.

At first, the Prayer may seem strange and a little difficult; but in time, it will become more comfortable as you learn to focus upon the heart, rather than all of the words. Through this example, you will learn how to use it for yourself. These words are guidelines only and what is most important is to speak your request from your feeling center.

1. Drop deeply into your heart. One way to access the deeper heart is to see yourself in your mind as a little child playing around in your thoughts. Suddenly, you get the idea you want try something different and go swimming in the pool of *love*, which is located in your heart. See yourself climb up on

the slide *(The top of the slide is in the mind and the bottom is in the heart)* and sit at the top of the slide for a moment, surveying the journey down the slope into your heart. *At this point, work to get into your feelings before letting go, for we switch hereafter from seeing/thinking to feeling. Focusing on something or someone that makes you feel good and warm inside will help you get into your feeling place.*

2. When you are ready, let yourself slide down into the big swimming pool full of *love*. Make it fun for yourself when you go down the slide—giggle and scream with excitement. When you splash into the pool of *love*, feel the iridescent pink water as it moves across your skin, making you tingle inside. Turn and float on your back or do whatever you desire before continuing. This will help to embody the experience. The deeper you are in your heart, the more profound will be your results.

3. While relaxing in the pink soothing fluid of your heart, look above you. There is a warm golden Light shining above your head. This represents your own I AM Presence. Take a moment to feel the warmth and love this Higher Aspect feels towards you, its Earth-self. Your I AM loves you no matter what. It does not judge and can only love. As you feel the embracing love of your Presence, located just a few feet above your body, notice that you are moving into an upright position. Suddenly, a beautiful Lotus flower emerges from the water holding your bare feet within its petals. *(The Lotus represents compassion and love and was brought here from Venus.)* Say these words, or something similar:

4. "I now call upon my beloved I AM Presence in great appreciation for all you have given unto me I make this call

in the name of my beloved Lord, Jesus Christ. *(Until you are fully connected, you must do it in **my** name so I can connect you to the Christ Grid and beyond. The day will come as you awaken fully that you will no longer need to call upon me for assistance.)* I know that I have done many things upon the Earth that have harmed humanity, as well as me. I did these acts out of forgetfulness of who I am and that my true nature is love. I have now become aware of _____ *(put the act that you want to have forgiven into this slot. For this exercise we will insert **hurtful words**.)* I do not wish to harm others and yet I have done so through my words. I wish to call forth the *Forgiveness Prayer* and ask that all the deeds I have done to others that may have caused them harm, real or imagined, be forgiven. I am now willing to stand accountable to my I AM Presence for these actions, even those I can't remember. I ask to be forgiven. *(Allow yourself to stay here in the Light and bask in the love of your I AM before going any further).*

5. I now ask Saint Germain, the Keeper of the Violet Flame *(flame of transmutation),* to send forth the violet energy to assist me. *(See it coming not only from St. Germain but also out of the palms of your I AM Presence. Visualize the Lotus flower bringing this same energy up around your feet and legs, washing your entire body. Saint Germain often will not appear in a form, but will only appear as the color of violet.)* I give thanks to you, Saint Germain, for your love and compassion and for holding this energy so that my actions might be transmuted through this flame. *(Saint Germain is overseeing the freedom energy for the next 2,000 years and was my father, Joseph, when I was upon the Earth.)* Beloved St. Germain, I ask that you transmute the words that I have

spoken in this lifetime and all others that have ever caused harm to another. I ask humanity to be cut free from any of my creations. Let people now have freedom from the harm that I did to them. Where there was pain, let there now be joy. Take this negative energy and transmute it and then do what you deem necessary with it. I also ask for myself that I too be freed from my belief in the human creations of pain and limitation. Cleanse and purify my throat chakra from this time forth. I ask that the transmutation energy continue to burn through me and around me for as long as it takes and all are brought back into their rightful state of peace and balance. With gratitude, I give thanks unto thee. Amen."

Stay in this energy however long it takes, until you feel ready to open your eyes. Know that the Flame of Transmutation will continue to burn through your discord until all is done. This does not mean you will not have to repeat the Prayer as a deeper layer of awareness arises. This process can be used for everything in your life, as well as in others' lives. Remember, they are you. You cannot, however, use the Prayer in any way for harm of another.

I would like to do a brief recap of the steps, so you can memorize them if you like. Remember, the key is calling the Prayer forth from the heart, your feeling center.

1. Drop into the heart.
2. Call upon your I AM; give thanks to this part of yourself for being there for you.
3. State what you want *forgiveness* for and stand accountable for all of your actions.
4. Call forth the Violet Flame, St. Germain.

5. Ask all discord done to others and to yourself be transmuted, and where there was pain, ask that there now be joy.
6. Give thanks for this assistance in the name of Lord Jesus Christ and close your Prayer.

I would like to share another example of how the *Forgiveness Prayer* might be used. Let us say you were in a store and suddenly you saw an angry mother yelling at her child. Being aware how words can harm, you decide immediately you will use the Prayer. However, as you pray, remember she **is** you. So you ask that all of **your** angry words that have caused harm to others be forgiven and transmuted. **She is in your awareness because she is the mirror for you**. Once you take accountability, everything changes. Once the Prayer is complete, the energy around the situation will begin to change. With practice, you will be able to stop right where you are and offer this Prayer silently. It does not need to take a long time. The more you practice it, the easier it becomes. The more you do it, the freer you become from all of the chains that have bound you. The heart is what opens up the gates for the cleansing to occur. (Of course, this scenario applies for both genders.)

When prayers such as this are offered, they not only affect you and the person who reflected the issue, but also the prayer moves out into all of the energy fields of the planet, affecting all of humanity. People begin to heal because of Unity Consciousness. Ascension is assured for the one who learns to master his/her own discord. The battle in these last days, my brothers and sisters, is not the battle you have feared in the outward world; it is the battle within that strikes fear in your heart.

Discord is built out of fear; it is built out of jealousy. If you are jealous of others, I ask you to look inside and see what you are not giving to you. If you have judgment over another, I ask you where is it that you do not love yourself? Where are you judging yourself? Everyone is a mirror of you. Therefore, instead of focusing outward during this last battle—often referred to as *Armageddon*, but I prefer to call it as *the time of great transformation*—**focus within and you will be triumphant.**

You are being called forth now to live the Higher Law—the Law within yourself of *accountability*; the Law within yourself to master the jealousies, the anger, the victimhood within yourself. As you summon back your power to understand your life, you will move out of discord into this tube of Light to align with your own Divinity, and thereby, you will pass from the discord. Only you can make that call, my brothers and sisters.

Know that you are love. Choosing to lay down the discord and to return to what you know yourself to be is the only way you can pass through this. I offer these teachings so you can begin to understand yourselves. In addition, I offer simple tools to help dissolve discord:

1. **Your solar plexus**: Or your **power-center** is a place where anger and discord can enter. This is also a place that is easily psychically attacked by those in form and out of form (*Entities*). This **third chakra** is where your power lies, so therefore, it is one of the first places that the *shadow* will go after. If this happens to you, immediately call me forth to shield this area for you and to shine my Light on your behalf. Also by crossing your legs and putting your hands over the solar plexus, you help to push away anything trying to enter. It is important to immediately drop into your heart and feel love, for this stops *shadow-energy* from entering.

You may want my assistance with fights, violence, extreme anger, fear, cross words with your mate, and road-rage. Call for me.

2. **Blue is the color of the Divine Will**. The **Cross** is my symbol and has the meaning of Creation associated with it. **Where two points intersect, Creation begins**. Visualize in your mind a blue cross that is bigger than your body. See yourself right in the center of the cross. See it growing larger and larger until you begin to feel small within it. As the energy grows, the cross ignites a field of energy around you that creates a force field of protection. The symbol of the cross is the Divine Will; you and I are creating a new field of Creation for you to live within; one in which peace and protection reside.

3. Never hesitate to call upon me for all things, my Beloveds, for there is nothing too big or too small you cannot enlist my help with. When you sleep, ask me to cover you with my blanket of radiating love. Invite me into your heart when there is pain. I will walk with you through all of life's difficulties.

Your brother Jesus—Jeshua ben Joseph

SIDEBARS

Front Cover: Jesus/Jeshua has said that he wanted humanity to get him off the cross, so I asked him if he wanted the Maltese cross deleted from the cover. He answered in a firm NO, and the following is his explanation: *"I want to get off the cross in the way humanity has me, for the true meaning of the cross is characterized and symbolic of **two points of Light that cross** each other, signifying Creation; it must be understood that is different from the cross that humanity has placed me upon. That cross has represented death, and yet the origination of the two points is **life!**"*

Prologue: *"The purpose for stating it this way is so that as people read the beginning Prologue, they will begin to understand more of what this book is about. This book is about many aspects of truth and the various ways of viewing what people have heard. The book's purpose is to bring them into a state where they will start to question within themselves. They will feel the truthfulness, for within each chapter, the truths that are spoken cannot help but pull at the heart strings of those who are reading it."* (The names of the two sisters were not stated so that the Beloveds would remain focused on Jesus' words, versus shifting their attention to these Biblical women.)

Introduction: *"I do not give specific timelines, names, and scientific data because there are others who are doing that in their books. Actually, what I wish this book to be is a story of humanity, and my part and your part in it. It is hoped then that humanity can finally get me off the pedestal."* (Jesus/Jeshua ben Joseph's name is spelled with a **J** for this book per his request. Spelling it with a Y evokes the Hebrew energy of yesteryears.)

Chapter 1—Ye Are Gods: Cynthia asked Jesus, "Would you be willing to tell me what it feels like to have the Father's Energy flow through you?"

Jesus: *Ahhh, as It runs through your veins, It's like a soothing liquid gold that makes your body feel all warm inside from the Light. It is all encompassing, and every place that It touches begins to glow with the feeling of unconditional love. It's so powerful that It feels like the grand finale on the 4ᵗʰ of July going off inside of you, all at once. Of course there are really no words to describe It, for It's an inexplicable experience!"*

Chapter 2—The Treasure Chest: We all have played out, or are currently playing out, our alcohol games. I (Chako) was a wino in a past life. In this lifetime, I began to notice a pattern with wine. Approximately 6 hours after a dinner party and the consumption of various wines, I would become violently ill at both ends! When I finally made the connection and stopped wines and then any liquor, period, I no longer became ill from a dinner party. It takes more than one lifetime to end one's alcohol games. I have learned my lesson and have ended that game! Thank you, Elementals.

Through my own illness (Cynthia) these last two years in completing this book with Chako, I had to learn to work in a deeper way with my elementals. They became very focused on **their** well being and not what I wanted if I desired to stay upon the Earth. I could no longer consume many of the foods I used to eat. For the most part, I was only allowed to eat *greens*. When I asked them *why*, they told me there was a switch-over occurring. The elementals in my body were being upgraded and a different way of eating was now in order to support the Light that my body was changing into. I cannot say it was easy in the beginning stages because I did not understand. How grateful I am today as they have taught me to be more present, as well as grateful for their work. I am learning now how to co-create with them.

Chapter 3—Heavenly Assistance: *Understand that there is imprinting being done. It is not so much the words, but the energy that the pages hold. Each time one awakens, the imprint is carried to the world to help other inhabitants awaken. In Oneness, it can be no other way. "Where two or more are gathered together, there is great movement upon the Earth." That is why* **two** *channels were used, Jeshua said in writing this book. Jeshua stated, "I am in the unseen world right now, but the two of you are in the seen realm, and it requires two to be in the physical realms in order to bring about this shift (Jesus 2013)."*

Cynthia had difficulty working with this chapter. She had one delay after another, mainly from her beloved dog, Yoda, who suffered from a tick bite, causing him to bite a hole in his tail. After that, 3 spider bites. Still she could not pick up the rhythm in order to complete the editing that was required. Frustrated, she asked Jeshua why she could not complete the work required on this chapter. He replied, *have you found the virtue in this experience yet*?

She awoke the next morning knowing her lesson was *detachment* and the virtue is *compassion for self*. She sent the chapter off to me at 3:00 AM, completed.

Chapter 4—The Energy of Discord: A student asked Jeshua what to do when family members or others are doing their covertness and manipulation creating discord. He replied to just back away and find humor in the drama. *Oh, isn't that interesting; the person(s) is afraid to be on the surface, afraid to be seen. He/she must create discord covertly.* And so they do.

Jeshua continues teaching: If there is covertness going on and it is in your direct energy fields, somewhere inside of you, you are being covert within yourself. That may mean you are not willing to see something about yourself. So you keep pretending that it is not there. You will know your inner work is successful when the covertness against you turns to overt-ness. The person(s) will say it right to your face. However, many families were raised to not confront and to be covert, for it was not safe to do otherwise. It is in their DNA. You cannot blame them from the DNA stand point, for if you spoke your truth, you could be beheaded, have your arms cut off, been raped, thrown into the stocks, any number of things. Therefore, **it could be in your family line to be covert.**

What is happening is that the person(s) could be living out covertly because it was never safe to speak the truth. In this way, you do not have to be attached to the drama of it; back away and see it for what it is. In this manner, **you** are choosing neither to be covert with your own actions nor to judge the situation you actually stopped—discord—from occurring. You then become a part of the solution rather than contributing to the problem.

This also helps you to stop being covert in the inner realms. Every time you judge another's action, you are creating discord whether for that person, or within yourself. Humanity is learning how to speak its truth. Even though many are awakening to their truth, there are still acts being done in a covert way due to fear of being persecuted if they dare speak up. This dynamic is soon to change at a very rapid speed. What a welcome relief it will be for the truth to be spoken in each moment. You will know where everyone stands. Everyone will become his/her true authentic self.

Chapter 5: Lucifer's Gift & The Dark Seed: *The truth is all of this came about because Lucifer and I were given different assignments. Lucifer was given the assignment to divide and conquer and to know the male side and its strength. Strength is the male side. I (Jesus/Jeshua, a female soul) was given the assignment to teach the feminine and to work things out through communication. Females carry the power. Therefore, the two sides had to come into balance with one another. That is the only way polarity integration could take place. One had to take the softer role (me); one had to take the harder role (Lucifer). That is why I speak of the diamond mine. Only under pressure, the harsher role, can one refine the diamond within. That is Lucifer's role—to help you mine your diamond. It is important for both parts to work in tandem—power with strength.*

The Dark Seed: The Victorian house depicted in Chako's story was purchased by her parents, partially furnished, and mortgaged for $4000 in 1933 or so. Her father, Karlton Kimball Priest, DDS, and her mother, Ethel Dare Humphrys Priest, MD, moved into the house when Ethel was 44 and she died there when she was 94 in 1986. Chako sold the house a few years later and the new owner redecorated it in the Victorian-Italian style. The house can be seen on the Internet under Bed-Breakfast, Napa, CA. Click on McClelland-Priest B and B Inn and visit her childhood's home. (569 Randolph St., Napa, CA 94559)

Chapter 6—Moving from Duality to Oneness: There are more than 2000 strands of DNA and that is still a small number. Jesus: *I will stretch you further. What creates the neutral energy that I speak* *of? No one really knows, for it has always been so. There are many levels to Heaven and many undiscovered secrets that are not known, even to me. Why is that so, because there are many Gods and many levels to God. It is a difficult concept for humanity to grasp that there is no beginning and ending. It has just always been.*

Chapter 7—Illuminated Obedience: (*The following is from Jesus' lecture channeled by Cynthia and given at Chako's house in Surprise, AZ, 9-19-10.*) The fourth dimension (4D) is where your disembodied Etheric Beings reside and 4D is deep into the Reptilians and Grays. This is the level of mind-control. The third dimension (3D) is what you have out-pictured—the world you have lived in. 3D is creation in density. The fourth is where your mind is either going to be set free or controlled. The fifth dimension (5D) is where there is the beginning of real *freedom*. The fourth is not free; it is on your way to freedom. However, 4D is not as dense as the 3D reality.

There are many different ways of controlling. If it were not so, there would be peace upon the Earth right now. Transformation is taking place within humanity right now. The more humanity finds its Illuminated Truth, the faster it can pass into 5D. One can be in 5D and be among 4D people. What will catapult you to 5D is *joy.* Humanity is not in joy, but back in 3D—with the white picket fence and the Tupperware parties. Soon this will all change.

There are pockets of dark energy that get freed up at different times. Some of these dark energies are from the past—Egypt, for example. The result can be an **increase of scorpions** in the southern regions of America. Or on a more personal level you might experience a rash of flat tires on your vehicle. **Flat tires are indicative to a lack of movement**, not moving forward in your life.

Bizarre happenings can and will occur. A large tree branch can crash just in front of you. The tree is releasing an energy that has been blocking you. You are always kept safe when you are within your Illuminated Self. Please understand that any energy that is released goes not only into the atmosphere, but into the Earth herself if it is not transmuted. So this is why I have provided the examples spoken of to show you how these energies can be released, for in Oneness there are no accidents.

Discord comes also from things humanity is doing to the Earth. An example is where instruments are placed within the Earth—such as the machinery in Switzerland or in other various regions of the Earth—to emit sonic sounds, which are disruptive to people' and animals' energy fields. The important thing to remember always is not to go into fear, no matter what goes on around you. Do not buy into the discord. By the end of the year 2012 and beyond, time will have sped up to such an extent that you will think a thought and it will manifest. Do you want healing? See yourself healed. Do not see what it is you think you have at the current moment, unless it is dis-ease you want to create. It is that simple. Only see what it is you desire. And you will have it because you will bring your Light bodies into alignment, which allows the creation to manifest. (2013)

You have the ability right now to change time-lines. You may already have noticed this. There are multiple time-lines, as well as previous lives, folding in on one another. Many of you are passing through various lives. **Not all of you are on the same page.** Mother Earth, as a whole, is passing through the time-line of Egypt—hence the increase of scorpions. There are certain things that are occurring in the fourth dimension that were very much a part of the captivity of humanity's mind during Egyptian times.

Others of you will be passing through the time-lines of Lemuria, and some of you are passing through the time-lines of Atlantis. However, as you pass through them, you will have a collapsing of various life events. Think of an ocean wave making its way to shore. Each breaker brings a past life to your body and exposes what is still to be transmuted. You can choose through your thoughts to switch time-lines. You can choose through your intention to be whatever it is you want to be. If you focus on a younger body, if you focus on good health, if you focus on the things that you desire, my Beloveds, you can change without drama. (2013)

During the Question & Answer period of the class, I, Chako, asked Jeshua what it would mean for my grandson, Jason Smallwood, who would be seven years of age on the auspicious date of 10-10-10. *My beloved, he is a brilliant star. Look out as he grows older. He has great work to do upon the Earth. He will be catapulted tremendously ahead. He has come as a great way-shower for the family.*

Jeshua was asked if we focused on anything we desired and saw it in front of us, whether we could just breathe it in for manifestation. *That is one way, if you can let it in.* Q: What does one do in order to let it in? A: *Illuminate yourself. You see, if you do not believe in that, if you do not have faith in that, you are at another level of belief and that may be difficult for people. However, if you know through these teachings, and you desire to be healed, and you are in tune with your Higher-Self, you will be healed.*

Understand that any discord in the body is nothing but bottled-up energy. Say to yourself when you have this bottled up energy: "it is time to love me—all of me. I choose to let go of all the pain that I am suffering in this lifetime. I choose that all the pain I might have inflicted upon others be freed from them." Feel this happening with

*an open heart. As it is freed from them, then it is freed from you and
then all will return to love.*

There are certain **thought forms** that take the position of Beings
within the physical form. They do not reside very well with love and
accountability. As you drop deeper and deeper within the heart, you
no longer can hold the discord in your body in the same way. This
discord is what causes so much pain and physical distress in a body.
When you are in gratitude, the discord must leave.

The discord that is out-picturing, meaning that it is coming back
to the Earth, is coming back to you as a person or back upon the Earth
as the mass consciousness. (Remember, **25% of karma is yours;
the other 75% is mass consciousness—humanity's.**) A good bit of
what is/will be occurring on Earth is from **mass consciousness**.

The Heavens want nothing for you but for you to have everything
that you want. But we cannot give this to you until you understand that
it is your negativity, the discord that must be neutralized—released
in order for the blessings to come. Gratitude says to the discord:
*Move aside; move aside; I am in gratitude for everything in my life.
I am in gratitude for the discord for it has showed me what I have
believed in that is not true.*

There is so much fear in the human consciousness that has been
released. As it is released, it goes into a band around the Earth and is
held; otherwise it would destroy the Universe. It is held there until
such time that it must come back to the Earth to be re-synthesized.
Consequently, as you open your own hearts and do your own
Forgiveness Prayer, and as you call forth in gratitude, you can bring
forth a shift of the energy that is already lying out there getting ready
to come back to the Earth. You can help still that energy so that it
comes back in a different way.

Thereby, as you follow it with your hearts, as you follow it with your gratitude, as you follow it with all that you do to bring more love and Light into your life with gratefulness, the energy that was laying there becomes neutralized. What then comes back is a much softer, abundant energy for humanity. Consequently, the ride will be much easier into the New World.

Many prophecies have been made about difficulties upon the planet, and yet many of those did not take place. It was not that they did not exist in the Etheric blue-print—the Akashic—but because those who knew the Law of Transformation knew that through gratitude, through shifting and using the Violet Energy, one could change all things. Thus the Masters went to work until enough of humanity awakened to understand that **you** could do this too. As the Heavens held this intent, they were able to give humanity a softer ride.

These last days are about **mastery of self**. The Ascension is about mastering yourself. It is not about being saved. Do not doubt for a moment that we in the Heavens are there for you. At any time that you need an extra bit of help or you are putting forth a prayer of gratitude, ask all the Ascended Masters to bring their Energy of Light and love into your request. Can you imagine the out-picturing when you do that? We will come immediately and fuse our Energies in with your request. Many of you are here, as uncomfortable as it might be, because you are Light. What greater Light can you be as you exercise *gratitude*?

All of you are in a fluid state because you are coming into your Godhood. Therefore, what used to be locked in a box of understanding and beliefs is no longer that way. That is the whole purpose of the Garden story because the Garden had a certain way that it thought its needs had to be met, until it finally empowered itself and realized that in gratitude its needs are met.

190

So it is with you, my Beloveds; you are moving out of the Garden of Despair to your own Garden of Godhood. Your futures are what **you** want, not what we in the Heavens want. We in the Heavens want all of your dreams to come true. But they cannot come true until you realize who it is you are; or, you will stay in the Garden of Despair. Then in despair you will stay until you wake up that it is **you**. It is all about you. That is called the Ascension.

That is why you are here during this time, riding the waves of change, being with Mother Earth as she births herself into a new level. The rarity of that is unheard of—to have humans being a part of this birth. But your futures are fluid. What do you want? Focus. What do you desire? Focus. You all are mastering your abilities to bring to you what you desire.

Many of the Lightworkers on the Earth will have some difficulties, for while they say they are Lightworkers, a true Lightworker is mastering him/herself. Some have not done the work and so difficulties will arise. However, those of you who do the work can share with them. *This is how I got here; this is the work that I did; take this knowledge and use it how **you** like to create your own way.*

Those of you who have done a great deal of internal work may no longer be seen by others. Here is the reason: **the optic nerve will not be registering in the same way**. Remember you will be vibrating at a different frequency than another person. They will not be able to see or hear you in the same way due to the change in frequency. You can walk into a room and they may not acknowledge you, nor even see you. You can go into a restaurant and sit there with no waiter coming to take your order. However, at that moment you can make a conscious choice to be seen, so do not worry about family and friends. They will see you, if you so choose.

Chapter 8—The Building Blocks of Love—The Creation: Master Hilarion is Chohan of the 5th Ray. He was also Saint Paul's **father** in those Biblical times.

Did you realize that a mermaid or **merman** was one of the guardians of Earth? They are not just some mythical creature—they are very real. Those with spiritual sight can see them even today.

Chapter 9—The Value of Silence: A question was raised to Jeshua, as he gave this lecture, as to how a strict vegetarian could ingest more protein, especially after the person was recovering from surgery and an increase in protein is needed. *There are those who will not consume animal protein because of their belief structure around harming animals. However, there are times that if you place your hand over the protein and give thanks to the animal, even though it was killed in violence, you can thank that animal for its sacrifice for what it has done. That will free it of that experience within its own DNA. It is important for the body to receive the protein. A vegan needs to increase the amount of vegetable protein he/she is eating—beans, rice—whatever the person chooses. Protein is still needed in your flesh body in order to move to the next vibrational level of life.*

Another example would be when you are building a house. You first must put in the stem walls in order to give the drywalls something to hang onto. In this next level of growth, you are building your "stem walls" and infusing that with good protein for the time being. Then you will fill this with Light—much more Light than you had before.

You will find that your food intake will change again where you will not want protein in the same way you have been eating it. You will consume lots and lots of vegetables, for you will be putting in the "drywall." Once that is established, the next level of Light infusion will be where you will no longer need animal protein but you will need a different type of plant protein. And that is enough to hold the "stem walls." Also, as you move more into the template of the plant protein, your consumption of sugar should wane because sugar takes you back down into the density.

Light will allow you to manifest more quickly. Do not focus on what you do not have but on what you desire, for this is what this next structure of your building will bring forth. Your manifestation is going to speed up.

A question was put forth during Jeshua's teaching as to why healers are unable to heal themselves many times—was it because they do not have compassion for themselves? *There are many things involved here. Here is an example: When you go to school to become a fireman, someone could say, "How come they cannot put out their own fires?" Understand what you teach; you go into training in order to learn how to do what you need to do for yourself. There are many healers who can heal others but cannot heal themselves.* Jeshua went on teaching his class. *It is a life-long journey. Every one of you in this room is a healer. There is not one of you who is not. However, you have varying degrees in your ability to heal yourself. That does not mean you do not have wisdom to impart to another while you are learning. This is why healers still have to work on themselves. When they work on some issue within themselves, then they are able to glean the understanding and are able to help another. Every true healer knows the journey to healing is to work upon him/herself so that healing for others may take place.*

The student questioned further if it were possible to work on another and not work on him/herself. *It is possible because the angels still work through different people to help bring about the best for them. Therefore, healers may summon from the heart, but still have areas within their own body that are diseased or in discord. That does not mean that their call is not heard when it comes from the heart.*

A healer's soul contract will go only so far, and perhaps his desire in this lifetime is not to fully heal himself. It could be similar to a Being that desires to journey and master him/herself and return to Source in order to bring that Source energy into the Earth. That is no better or worse than someone's declaring that he/she is not ready to go back to Source in this lifetime because he/she still wants to play in this Earth playground. Therefore, "I will go just to this point, for there are many people who need help to this point." Then someone else steps in and takes the person to another level for his/her healing.

The end result then is the healer's soul contract is not completed. He/she lives out the soul contract by giving, but not the soul's work so that in another lifetime, the work can continue. Not everyone wants to go to the same place, but everyone will ascend to some degree. Not everyone goes to college and takes the same courses and comes out with the same degree. People study different courses in order to learn different things. However, everyone in the college can still impart wisdom, according to what learning curve he/she is experiencing.

*It is similar to mediumship. **There are 33 levels to channeling**. It does not mean that information that comes through this vehicle (Cynthia) is not valid. We bring the information through that needs to be brought at the level where she is. As the vehicle changes and she works on herself—her own thoughts, her own processes—that will allow more Light in so that the Hosts of Heaven are more able to come through her body in an even purer way.*

A question was raised as to what knowledge the Druids imparted to Jesus during the time that he studied with them. *There is not a teaching upon the Earth at that time that I did not study because all of it was different aspects of Creator Energy.*

A student asked for information on how to build up the immune system. *Obtain Colostrums at a health food store. Vitamin D-3 is very important for building up the immune system as well.*

There are going to be so many people, including in your own families who will not hear your knowledge and wisdom. This is when you practice "loving allowance" that Dr. Peebles (Cynthia's Gate Keeper) speaks about. Be in loving allowance for the journey people are taking. This is also part of your mastering yourself, for you have so much information you could give and yet your lips must remain sealed until someone asks for it.

You can make a suggestion to a family member, but thereafter, you must allow the person his/her journey, because everyone is experiencing and exercising free will right now. That dynamic is foremost for humanity—in a big way! People are seeking their own truth and path; therefore they do not want anyone else to tell them what their truth is unless it is solicited. Always remember that a person's Higher-Self has a say in all of the drama.

To learn more about the value of Silence, Father took me, Cynthia, into a year of nothing but Silence. I was in a strange state and city. I had no friends and was too sick to socialize. I had a full year to study the teachings of this book and this chapter on Silence through living it. I can tell you there is nothing quite like this depth of silence where all you really have is the Heavens to depend on to get you through the days.

Chapter 10—The Many Faces of Joy & For the Love of Animals:
Sara, Chako's youngest daughter, is an accomplished equestrian rider (and now judge), and watching her compete in the Pan American Equestrian games some years ago brought much joy, as a Mom, to see her daughter excel in such a difficult and dangerous sport.

And Susan, Chako's eldest daughter became a widow when she was only in her 30's. As she picked herself up and continued going to work every day to become a stabilizing factor for her two young sons, it brought her mother such joy to see the inner strength of her beloved, grieving daughter.

I, Cynthia, have always told people that I could not have made it to this stage in my own development of finding God and a deeper connection with Jeshua without the help of my animals. Throughout my entire life, I have had a dog to help guide me. (Know that I have always loved Jeshua and had spoken with him since I was a child, but not in the way I do now.)

One of my dogs, Mookie, in her passing had told me as she was dying that she thanked me for having given her such a good life. She had three roads she could have taken to learn her lessons. Because I had rescued her—she was abandoned upon the streets, and I loved her so much—she was able to grow and develop in ways she could not have if she had taken the other two roads. This allowed her to heal her own abandonment, which would now allow her to journey much deeper into Heaven.

I really did not understand any of this at the time. However, during her last few hours of dying, she shared with me that she was going to give back to me by taking the energy cords of my heart with her. Again, I did not understand the depth of what she was talking about. After her death, I felt a tug on my heart and I could feel her swimming as fast as she could upward into the deeper places of

Heaven. I suddenly exploded in my crown chakra and heard all of humanity talking at the same time. It was profound, but I still did not understand.

I realize now what she was doing. She took my energy right back into the Heart of God. It was several months later that she returned to talk with me. She told me it took her a while to go that deep into Heaven. This allowed me to climb Jacob's ladder all the way back to God, if I so chose.

She now helps animals as they pass from one plane to the next, so they do not get lost. She told me that there is a very special place that is reserved just for animals where they can run all day long and play. The fairies are there and it is filled with joy and pure love. It is like a holiday when they have finished their work upon the Earth. It is here that they heal and recoup before they go on to the next mission that they are given in service of God. If you have a pet that is passing, you can call upon her. Her name is *Mookie Williams*.

I would be amiss if I did not mention my last dog that has journeyed with me through this intense illness to transform my body into a new vibration. His name is *Yoda*. Our journey has been profound. He loved me when I had no strength to attend to his needs. I awoke one night to see him eating a paper bag because he was so hungry. I did not realize, due to my body's pain, that I had not fed him. Who knows how long it had been. He still wagged his tail, however, and sat beside me and never judged me. He took on some of the sores that my body was purging to help me transmute them. He walked every step of the way with me through this last year and a half with such dedication.

He knew I would make it even if I did not. I know he kept me fighting. I knew if I died, there was no one to take him because I was living in an area where I knew no one and had been too sick to meet anyone. I also know that when he had fought so hard to help me, if I gave up now, he would be left with the energy of *abandonment*. As sensitive as he is, that would wound him and he would have to come back again to heal that hurt. I did not want that for him. I know how hard it has been for me to heal my own wounded heart. How wise Yoda is because he knew that would keep me fighting also. By the way, he named himself *Yoda,* not me. He told me it was after a wise man that lived in the 1400's. Ah, through this journey he lives true to his name. I love you so, Yoda!

Chapter 11—The Value of Gratitude: It will do much to soften humanity's journey if you will call forth the Forgiveness Prayer each day because of all of the thought-forms of pain and anguish that are there. (*See the Appendix for this Prayer.*) Remember the story about the Garden of Despair and what a simple solution there would be for unhappiness if humanity just would accept life with gratitude and thereby reap the gifts that await.

Jeshua has asked me (Cynthia) to read the *Value of Gratitude* and the *Garden of Despair* story over and over again as I transform my body into these new vibrations. He told me that the book, but especially these two stories, is loaded with an unspoken energy to help all who read it to heal the deeper places within their own hearts.

Chapter 12—My Love of the Sea: Cynthia wrote this during a period of intense illness from shingles around the right eye and forehead—October, 2011-June, 2012. Jeshua healed her eye so that she did not lose her sight, but the healing of her total body was up to her as part of *Master Yourself.* She is still healing and mining her diamonds. He told her she would heal more quickly now that the book is finished. "The book was completed and I, for one, was relieved. I was just coming out of the *diamond mine* and things were still difficult for me as I was also dealing with a lot of pain and no strength.

Jeshua began talking with me about what he wanted to add to chapter 12. At first I told him this could not be done; the book was being printed as we spoke. I immediately called Chako and told her what he was telling me and her first thought was the same as mine—oh NO! I told her what Jeshua had said and that all would get taken care of, for he wanted it revised. She then found out that the publisher was offering a special promotion for revisions and it was not too soon to do one. That was the answer we needed, so a new publishing contract was drawn up. It did get worked out, just like Jeshua had said it would. (2013)

I personally think that because I was so ill during the writing of the last chapter, he did not give as much information as he wanted. I just could not do it and he did not want to push me. However, he did want the book out; so he cut the last chapter short. The timing had something to do with gateways, so the book had to be written and out within a *doorway* that had opened and would be closing shortly. It is beyond my understanding, as most of this book has been."

The rewrite on the book began in September of 2012 and was completed just before the November 28th gateway opened. He said these vibrations needed to be constructed, for they now carry the last of what will help humanity climb aboard the energetic bridge to cross from the old paradigm into the new. He could not complete the bridge until I had finished most of my own transformation, for it was coming out/through me and onto the paper.

Also in November, Chako was sent to Paradise Island-Nassau (Nov. 20-24) to do work with Atlantis of Antiquity—to hold the focus on Love, Joy, and Gratitude. This was combining with the final stages of my writing these additions for this next gateway. I am sure as time goes on, we both will see the reason for all of this and what it means in the bigger picture for humanity.

READER'S NOTES

PAGE:

EPILOGUE—CYNTHIA

I wish I could say this book was a breeze for me to do. However, it was not. I don't know if living the teachings would have had to take place if we were not in this time period upon the planet. However, I can say that I lived through what was written and experienced every inch of it on a very personal level.

There was one point when I was so ill and so angry that Jeshua/Jesus showed up and told me to reread what he had given as the Higher Commandments. Of course, I did not want to hear this at that particular time.

In my journey, I faced every fear imaginable in order to master myself. Jeshua spoke about this when he was making his point about the diamonds being mined from deep underground. I got to mine my own diamond field and bring these fears into the Light so they could heal.

Now that all is done, I can say that I live the teachings that he taught and will continue to live them. I learned about the importance of caring for your vehicle (your body) as well as loving oneself. So I have greatly benefited from his book.

At one point, I told Chako that this book had become my own textbook on life. Every time I came up against something, Jeshua would pull the book out and show it to me.

I thank you for reading it, and I hope you can glean something from it that will serve you in your life. It truly has served me in my own healing process.

EPILOGUE—CHAKO

Dear Beloveds, here is the long awaited book. As you have read in Cynthia's Epilogue, it was not an easy flow of energy. There were times that she wanted to throw THE BOOK back at Him, and there were times I wanted to throw THE BOOK back at her!

We started this book two years ago in June 2010. I reference my books by linear time and am used to bringing them to fruition in 3 to 6 months. As the months ticked by and then years with a yo-yo effect procedure, my frustration would rev up. My compassion for Cynthia's health issues with one crisis after another waned thin. My patience-mode also was taxed to the hilt.

I recognized my anger for what it was—loss of control of the timing of the book's completion. Arch Angel Michael pointed this out to me in a public setting (11-11-11) from which I returned home with a bruised ego. It took me several days to process all of the implications.

One of the ways that helped me was to reread the *Prologue* where Jeshua told of the contract that the 3 of us had and the promise that he had made to us way back when. I then would go within my sacred heart and from that place look deeply at my emotions and see how ego had a stranglehold on how the book should progress. I was to let go of the attachment to the timing of the book's publication . . . and rev up my compassion and patience modes.

Cynthia phoned me on Sunday, June 10, 2012 to let me know that she would have the last chapter finished by that week. (Jeshua had given her a firm nudge to do so.) And to use an old cliché, "the rest is history."

I found it rather amusing when Cynthia turned the **control** of the book back to me. (Look out what you pray for—you might get it!) I now had to spend hours getting the book ready to send to Trafford Publishing. Luckily, Heather, our editor, and I had already spent long hours going over the numerous files, as did Jeshua and I, rereading each one in order to make any changes—to add or to subtract.

Beloveds, you have read from Cynthia and me about the struggles, the health issues, the emotional pain, and the conflicts of interest that we both went through in birthing this project, or *Jeshua's Book*, as we call it. (He thinks of it as *Humanity's Book*.) Please realize that this book most likely will bring **your** diamond mine to the forefront so that you too can glean what you have hidden in its depths. At least this is what Jeshua is hoping for you. Take time to process each chapter and to listen to your inner voice, for you hold your own answers to your queries.

We three bless you for reading our book and may it bless you back in ways that may astound you!

Once again, thank you for reading this new revised edition. I know you will enjoy the new information Jeshua has brought forth.

Blessings, Chako (2013).

LIST OF BOOKS

Verling CHAKO Priest, Ph.D.
The Ultimate Experience, the Many Paths to God series:

BOOKS 1, 2, & 3 REVISITED (2011)

ISBN # 978-1-4269-7664-3 (sc)

ISBN# 978-1-4269-7665-0 (e-book)

REALITIES of the CRUCIFIXION (2006)

ISBN # 1-978-4669-2148-1

MESSAGES from the HEAVENLY HOSTS (2007)

ISBN # 1-4251-2550-6

YOUR SPACE BROTHERS and SISTERS GREET

YOU! (2008) ISBN # 978-1-4251-6302-0

TEACHINGS of the MASTERS of LIGHT (2008)

ISBN # 978-1-4251-8573-2

PAULUS of TARSUS (2010)

ISBN # 978-1-4669-209-1 (sc)

ISBN # 978-1-4669-2090-3 (e-book)

THE GODDESS RETURNS to EARTH (2010)

ISBN # 978-1-4269-3563-3

ISBN # 978-1-4269-3564-0 (e-book)

Available at Trafford: 1-888-232-4444, or, Amazon.com

www.godumentary.com/chako.htm.

Rev. Cynthia Williams & Verling CHAKO Priest, Ph.D.

By **Rev. Cynthia Williams**

THE EYE of the DOLPHIN: A Reluctant Journey to
Spiritual Awakening and Weirdness (2008)
heartdolphin.cw@gmail.com.
Jeshuabridgetolove@gmail.com

ABOUT THE AUTHOR—CYNTHIA

Cynthia Williams is a Trance Medium/Intuitive Spiritual Counselor who uses her gifts to aid and encourage others to find their own truths. She has an intense passion for the sea and all of its life forms. She also has a great love for animals. Often you will hear her say, "I am a mother of six children, three of whom are human and three of which are fur children." Then she giggles. She has suffered the loss of both human and fur children, so she understands the pain associated with the disconnect from one world to the next. However, she still considers herself to be a mother of six and will tell anyone who asks, "Once a mother, always a mother, and just because they have passed through a doorway to another realm does not mean I have forgotten them."

Cynthia has been following the teachings of Jeshua ben Joseph—Jesus—for many years. When she was a small child, he would come to her and sit beside her on the bed. She knew him only as Jesus then. Cynthia's father was a police officer and not very sensitive to a young girl's needs. This caused her much pain and confusion. During Jesus' visits, they would talk about her father's anger and her mother's fear. Cynthia thought everyone had these kinds of talks with Jesus. It never occurred to her to ask if this was normal, because it had always been this way.

It was not until her adulthood that something occurred that led her to realize this was not normal. She was trying very hard at this time to fit in with others. She was scared people would find out she possessed these gifts. In her attempt to normalize herself, Cynthia quit talking to Jesus. This only lasted for a period of 10 years. Her heart could no longer bear being without her friend.

When she called upon him again, he came and sat with her. He then explained to her that from now on she should address him as Jeshua ben Joseph and not Jesus. As he sat with her, he reached into his heart and pulled out some heart energy and placed it into Cynthia's heart. He told her from this time on they would become as one in their desires.

Then about three years ago, Jeshua ben Joseph sought Cynthia out in a different way. He asked her to begin channeling him. At first she was shocked and resisted, but he explained he desired this because many had lost their way and had turned their backs on him as they were angry. He went on to say that they had so focused upon his death and worshiped him that they were missing the eternal truths of his relationship with them. He desired humanity to see him as a brother and not always associate him with the cross. He wants everyone to wake up to who he/she is and know that we are all one. So Cynthia agreed.

Cynthia now leads groups to the ocean to commune with the dolphins and experience Jeshua ben Joseph's great love of the sea. Cynthia gives lectures/ and teaches classes pertaining to mastery and what she learned while writing this book. She is also available to bring through messages from Jeshua on other subject matters as well. Cynthia has traveled internationally speaking on behalf of the sea. She has also channeled in world peace events allowing herself to be the vehicle through which Jeshua and others have spoken.

To find out more about booking Cynthia for an event, please e-mail her or call her. (See the following page.)

Rev. Cynthia Williams

Jeshuabridgetolove@gmail.com

Or

www.heartdolphin.cw@gmail.com.

1-928-717-2872

Or

PO Box 6884

Asheville, North Carolina 28816

ABOUT THE AUTHOR—CHAKO

Verling CHAKO Priest, PhD, was born in Juneau, Alaska, hence her name of Cheechako, shortened to just Chako by her mother, a medical doctor, and her father, an orthodontist. Chako was raised in Napa, CA. She attended the University of California at Berkeley where she met her future husband. Upon their marriage and after his training as a Navy pilot, they settled into the military way of life. They lived twelve years outside of the United States Mainland in various places, which included Hawaii, Viet Nam, Australia, and Greece. Little did she know that these exotic lands and peoples were preparing her for her spiritual awakening years hence.

After her husband's retirement from the Navy, they resettled in Napa, California. It was during this time that she returned to school at Berkeley and then transferred to Sonoma University where she earned her first two degrees in Psychology. Chako then entered the doctoral program at the Institute of Transpersonal Psychology (ITP), renamed Sophia University (2012), which is now located in Palo Alto, CA. She successfully completed that program which consisted of a Master, as well as the Doctorate in Transpersonal Psychology. Ten years and four degrees later she was able to pursue her passion for Metaphysical and New Age Thought—her introduction into the Realm of the Spiritual Hierarchy and the Ascended Lords and Masters.

In 1988, Dr. Priest moved to Minnetonka, Minnesota. She co-authored a program for Methodist Hospital called *Second Time Around* for those with recurring cancer. She, as a volunteer, also facilitated a grief group for Pathways of Minneapolis and had a private practice.

Rev. Cynthia Williams & Verling CHAKO Priest, Ph.D.

She studied with a spiritual group in Minnetonka led by Donna Taylor and the Teacher, a group of 5 highly developed entities channeled by Donna. The group traveled extensively all over the world working with the energy grids of the planet and regaining parts of their energies that were still in sacred areas waiting to be reclaimed by them, the owners. They climbed in and out of the pyramids in Egypt, tromped through the Amazon forest in Venezuela, rode camels at Sinai, and climbed the Mountain. They hiked the paths at Qumran, trod the ancient roadways in Petra, Jordan, and walked where the Master Yeshua walked in Israel.

The time came, November 1999, when Chako was guided to move to Arizona—her next phase of growth. This is where she found her beloved Masters, who in reality had always been with her. They were **all** ready for her next phase, bringing into the physical several books—mind-provoking books—telepathically received by her, from these highly-evolved, beautiful, loving Beings. Each book stretches her capabilities, as well as her belief systems. Nevertheless, it is a challenge she gladly embraces.

In June, 2012, she finished writing her tenth book, this one in collaboration with Cynthia Williams. Whether there will be a sequel to this book or Chako will write another book in the future, she does not know. Allow her to be in the NOW *(smile)*.

AND three months later Cynthia and Chako were busy doing a re-write on the entire book. There was so much more that Jeshua wanted in His book. He was working with different time-lines, portals, and gateways in order to place the energies to build a bridge of understanding between the old and the new. Let them know if you were able to cross over that bridge, hopefully with ease and Grace. (2013)

Comments AZCHAKO@AOL.COM.